An Apologeticall Narration

ROBERT S. PAUL

UNITED CHURCH PRESS

Philadelphia · *Boston*

Library of Congress Catalog Number : 63-21913

Printed in the United States of America

Preface

FOR MANY YEARS I have wanted to see the re-appearance of the *Apologeticall Narration,* mainly because of its regrettable omission from Williston Walker's *Creeds and Platforms of Congregationalism.* It is a very important document in Congregational history.

However, it was not until the United Church Press invited me to edit it somewhat less than two years ago that I began serious work on it, and was at once faced with a dilemma. To edit a small pamphlet of thirty-one pages would seem to be a fairly modest undertaking, and yet I became convinced that to re-publish the booklet with a few explanatory notes might do more to strengthen ecclesiastical prejudices than it would to clarify historical perspectives. How could readers give it a proper assessment unless the editor tried to describe the complicated political and constitutional struggle in which the original publication of the *Apologeticall Narration* was but one (albeit, a significant) incident? What did we know of the men who wrote it or stood behind it, or of the Westminster Assembly in which the appearance of this *apologia* played such an important part?

A fairly extended commentary seemed to be required, and at once we came upon unexpected problems, not the least of which has been the want of any full-length biographies of the Dissenting Brethren or their associates, and the remarkable lack of any recent factual and chronological account of the Westminster Assembly. The result of our research upon the original form of this historical essay was disastrous, and only by means of ruthless pruning have we been able to reduce it to manageable size. I recognize that the present commentary by no means meets the need for more adequate treatment of the Apologists, but I trust it will fill some of the gaps; and since we have had to delete a great deal of fascinating material on the Westminster Assembly, I cherish the hope that before too long (from somebody's pen) a fuller account of that very significant event may appear.

iii

My " Introduction " is deliberately placed after the text of the *Apologeticall Narration*. Its position in this volume should emphasize that it has a very limited purpose — to introduce the reader to the complicated religious and political events in which the pamphlet appeared, and it is offered in the hope that it will make the reading of the text itself more intelligible and less open to modern presuppositions and bias.

Undoubtedly there will be Congregationalists and Presbyterians who will resent any suggestion that there were "unavowed motives" in the Westminster Assembly which were neither theological nor religious. It is clear that in matters of political manipulation neither of the parties in the Assembly could teach the other very much, and one has a shrewd suspicion that they were no better and probably no worse than the Episcopal party which preceded and followed them into power. My emphasis on the "non-theological factors" is deliberate because a very important part of the church historian's task in the immediate future must be to help the denominations to face these hidden motives honestly — and if anyone is tempted to gloat, let him reflect upon the mote and the beam.

If I stand on the Congregational side of the seventeenth-century argument it is not because I believe that all the claims of the Dissenting Brethren were valid, but because in one important respect I believe they re-discovered a New Testament insight which remains central in present-day ecumenical discussions : the principle that authority in the Church must be according to the mind of Christ. Let me assure my Presbyterian friends that this book is presented in the sincere belief that only by frankly facing our *common* Reformed history honestly can we eventually reach the unity which was our concern in earlier centuries.

* * * * *

My own contribution to this work is a modest tribute to Mansfield College, Oxford, where my interest in Puritan studies was first kindled. It is offered in the hope that it may long be enabled to inspire young scholars from both sides of the Atlantic with the best of the Puritan tradition. It is also written with affection towards the Congregational Union of England and Wales through which I entered into the heritage of Word and Sacrament, and towards the

United Church of Christ in the United States of America through which I enjoy that heritage at the present time.

I wish to thank my friends, Dr. Douglas Horton and Dr. Truman B. Douglass, and Mr. Charles A. Butts of the United Church Press for first asking me to undertake the work. Without this incentive I doubt whether it would ever have become more than a pious hope.

Former members of my seminars in Puritanism at the Hartford Seminary Foundation also deserve my thanks, and especially two who have given practical help: the Reverend Hamish Smith of Scotland who, in addition to bibliographical services, tried to hold my English prejudices in check, and the Reverend Richard Hasler, who prepared the index, and (as a good Presbyterian) pulled my Congregational enthusiasms into proper perspective. I must also thank Arlene Hasler and Mrs. Sebold for typing my manuscript and Mrs. Stratton for extremely careful work in copy-editing.

Finally, an unrepayable debt is always due to my wife and family when I am writing a book, and particularly when I am writing on some aspect of the seventeenth century. It is difficult enough to live oneself in two centuries at the same time, but to have to live with such a person must be rather like trying to read Tennessee Williams with someone in orbit. What can I say? I cannot sincerely say that I am sorry, but I can honestly say that I am grateful.

1962   Hartford, Connecticut

To the Teachers and Students, Past and Present,
of
Mansfield College, Oxford

CONTENTS

Facsimile of the 1643

An Apologeticall Narration

THis Apologeticall Narration *of our Reverend and deare Brethren the learned Authors of it,* 'tis so full of peaceablenesse, modesty, and candour ; and withall, at this time so seasonably needfull, *as well towards the vindication of the Protestant party in generall, from the aspersions of* Incommunicablenesse *within it selfe, and* Incompatiblenesse *with* Magistracy ; *as of themselves in particular, both against misreportings from without, & some possible mistakings from within too : That however for mine own part I have appeared on, and doe still encline to the Presbyteriall way of Church Government, yet doe I think it every way fit for the Presse.*

Charles Herle.

AN
Apologeticall Narration,

HVMBLY SVBMITTED

TO THE
HONOURABLE HOUSES

OF
PARLIAMENT.

BY
Tho: Goodwin,
Philip Nye ,.
Sidrach Simpson,
Jer: Burroughes,
William Bridge.

LONDON,
Printed for ROBERT DAWLMAN.
M. DC. XLIII.

AN
APOLOGETICALL NARRATION
OF SOME
MINISTERS,
Formerly in Exile:
NOW
Members of the Assembly *of Divines.*

 UR eares have been of late so filled with a sudden and unexpected noyse of confused exclamations, (though not so expresly directed against us in particular, yet in the interpretation of the most, reflecting on us) that awakened thereby, we are enforced to anticipate a little that discovery of our selves which otherwise we resolved to have left to *Time* and *Experience* of our wayes and spirits, the truest Discoverers and surest Judges of all men and their actions.

And now we shall begin to make some appearance into publique light, unto whose view and judgements should we (that have hitherto laine under so dark a cloud of manifold mis apprehensions) at first present our selves, but the Supreame Judicatory of this Kingdome, which is and hath been in all times the most just and severe Tribunall

B   for

for guiltineſſe to appeare before, much more to dare to appeale unto; and yet withall the moſt ſacred refuge and *Aſylum* for miſtaken and miſ-judged innocence:

The moſt, if not all of us, had ten years ſince (ſome more, ſome leſſe) ſeverall ſetled Stations in the Miniſtery, in places of publique uſe in the Church, not unknown to many of your ſelves; but the ſinful evill of thoſe corruptions in the publique worſhip and government of this Church, which all doe now ſo generally acknowledge and decrie, took hold upon our conſciences long before ſome others of our brethren; And then how impoſſible it was to continue in thoſe times our ſervice and ſtandings, all mens apprehenſions will readily acquit us.

Neither at the firſt did we ſee or look further then the *dark part*, the evill of thoſe ſuperſtitions adjoyned to the worſhip of God, which have been the common ſtumbling block and offence of many thouſand tender conſciences, both in our own and our neighbour Churches, ever ſince the firſt Reformation of Religion: which yet was enough to deprive us of the publique exerciſe of our Miniſteries, and together therewith (as the watchfulneſſe of thoſe times grew) of our perſonall participation in ſome ordinances; and further expoſed us either to perſonall violence and perſecution, or an exile to avoid it: Which latter we did the rather chooſe, that ſo the uſe and exerciſe of our Miniſteries (for which we were borne and live) might not be wholly loſt, nor our ſelves remain
de-

debarred from the enjoyment of the Ordinances of Chrift, which we account our birth-right, and beft portion in this life.

This being our condition, we were caft upon a farther neceffity of enquiring into and viewing the *light part*, the pofitive part of *Church-worfhip* and Government; And to that end to fearch out what were the firft Apoftolique directions, pattern and examples of thofe Primitive Churches recorded in the New Teftament, as that facred pillar of fire to guide us. And in this enquirie, we lookt upon the word of Chrift as impartially, and unprejudicedly, as men made of flefh and blood are like to doe in any juncture of time that may fall out; the places we went to, the condition we were in, the company we went forth with, affording no temptation to byas us any way, but leaving us as freely to be guided by that light and touch Gods Spirit fhould by the Word vouchfafe our confciences, as the Needle toucht with the Load-ftone is in the Compaffe: And we had (of all men) the greateft reafon to be true to our own confciences in what we fhould embrace, feeing it was for our confciences that we were deprived at once of what ever was dear to us. We had no new Common-wealths to rear, to frame Church-government unto, whereof any one piece might ftand in the others light, to caufe the leaft variation by us from the Primitive pattern; We had no State-ends or Politicall interefts to comply with; No Kingdoms in our eye to fubdue unto our mould; (which yet will be coexiftent with the peace of any form of Civil Govern-

ment

ment on earth) No preferment or worldly refpects
to fhape our opinions for : We had nothing elfe to
doe but fimply and fingly to confider how to worfhip God acceptably, and fo moft according to his
word.

We were not engaged by Education or other-
wife to any other of the Reformed Churches ; And
although we confulted with reverence what they
hold forth both in their writings and practice, yet
we could not but fuppofe that they might not fee
into all things about worfhip and government, their
intentions being moft fpent (as alfo of our firft Reformers in *England*) upon the Reformation in Doctrine, in which they had a moft happy hand : And
we had with many others obferved, that although
the exercife of that Government had been accompanied with more peace, yet the Practicall part, *the
power of godlineffe* and the profeffion thereof,
with difference from carnall and formall Chriftians, had not been advanced and held forth among
them, as in this our owne Ifland, as themfelves
have generally acknowledged. We had the advantage of all that light which the conflicts of our
owne Divines (the good old Non-conformifts)
had ftruck forth in their times ; And the draughts
of Difcipline which they had drawn ; which we
found not in all things the very fame with the pra-
ctifes of the Reformed Churches ; And what they
had written came much more commended to us,
not onely becaufe they were our own, but becaufe
fealed with their manifold and bitter fufferings.
We had likewife the fatall mifcarriages and fhip-

wracks

wracks of the *Separation* (whom ye call *Brownists*) as Land-marks to fore-warn us of thofe rocks and fhelves they ran upon ; which alfo did put us upon an enquiry into the principles that might be the caufes of their divifions. Laft of all, we had the recent and later example of the wayes and practices (and thofe improved to a better Edition and greater refinement, by all the fore-mentioned helps) of thofe multitudes of godly men of our own Nation, almoft to the number of another Nation, and among them fome as holy and judicious Divines as this Kingdome hath bred ; whofe fincerity in their way hath been teftified before all the world, and wil be unto all generations to come, by the greateft undertaking (but that of our father *Abraham* out of his own countrey, and his feed after him) a tranfplanting themfelves many thoufand miles diftance, and that by fea, into a Wildernes, meerly to worfhip God more purely, whither to allure them there could be no other invitement. And yet we ftill ftood as unengaged fpectators, free to examine and confider what truth is to be found in and amongft all thefe, (all which we look upon as Reformed Churches) and this nakedly according to the word ; We refolved not to take up our Religion by or from any partie, and yet to approve and hold faft whatfoever is good in any, though never fo much differing from us, yea oppofite unto us.

And for our own congregations, we meane of *England* (in which thorough the grace of Chrift we were converted, and exercifed our Minifteries

long,

long, to the conversion of many others) We have this sincere profession to make before God and all the world, that all *that* conscience of the defilements we conceived to cleave to the true worship of God in them, or of the unwarranted power in Church Governours exercised therein, did never work in any of us any other thought, much lesse opinion, but that multitudes of the assemblies and parochiall congregations thereof, were *the true Churches and Body of Christ, and the Ministery thereof a true Ministery:* Much lesse did it ever enter into our hearts to judge them *Antichristian;* we saw and cannot but see that by the same reason the Churches abroad in *Scotland, Holland, &c.* (though more reformed) yet for their mixture must be in like manner judged no Churches also, which to imagine or conceive, is and hath ever been an horrour to our thoughts. Yea we alwayes have professed, & that in these times when the Churches of *England* were the most, either actually overspread with defilements, or in the greatest danger thereof, and when our selves had least, yea no hopes of ever so much as visiting our own land again in peace and safety to our persons; that we both did and would hold a *communion* with them as the Churches of Christ. And besides this profession, as a reall testimony thereof, some of us after we, actually, were in this way of communion, baptized our children in Parishionall congregations, and (as we had occasion) did offer to receive into the communion of the Lords Supper with us, some (whom we knew godly that come to visit us when we were

in

in our exile) upon that relation, fellowſhip, and commemberſhip they held in their pariſh Churches in *England*, they profeſſing themſelves to be members thereof, and belonging thereunto. What we have ſince our returne publiquely and avowedly made declaration of to this purpoſe, many hundreds can witneſſe, and ſome of our brethren in their printed bookes candidly do teſtify for us.

Mr. *Cheynett.* Riſe & growth of Socinia- niſme.

And as we alwayes held this reſpect unto our own Churches in this Kingdome, ſo we received and were entertained with the like from thoſe reformed Churches abroad, among whom we were caſt to live, we both mutually gave and received the right hand of fellowſhip, which they on their parts abundantly manifeſted by the very ſame characters and teſtimonies of difference which are proper to their own Orthodoxe Churches, and whereby they uſe to diſtinguiſh them from all thoſe ſects (which they tollerate, but not own) and all the aſſemblies of them (which yet now we are here ſome would needs ranke us with) granting to ſome of us their own Churches, or publique places for worſhip, to aſſemble in, where themſelves met for the worſhip of God at differing houres the ſame day: As likewiſe the priviledge of ringing a publique Bell to call unto our meetings: which we mention becauſe it is amongſt them made the great ſignall of difference between their own allowed Churches and all other aſſemblies, unto whom it is ſtrictly prohibited and forbidden, as *Guiciardine* hath long ſince obſerved: And others of us found ſuch acceptance with them, that in teſtimony there-

of

of they allowed a full and liberall maintenance annually for our Minifters, yea and conftantly alfo Wine for our Communions. And then we again on our parts, not onely held all brotherly correfpondency with their Divines, but received alfo fome of the members of their Churches (who defired to communicate with us) unto communion in the Sacraments and other ordinances, by virtue of their relation of memberfhip retained in thofe Churches.

Now for the way & practices of our Churches, we give this briefe and generall account. Our *publique worfhip* was made up of no other parts then the worfhip of all other reformed Churches doth confift of. As, publique and folemne prayers *for Kings and all in authority, &c.* the reading the Scriptures of the Old and New Teftament; Expofition of them as occafion was; and conftant preaching of the word; the adminiftration of the two Sacraments, Baptifme to infants, and the Lords Supper; finging of Pfalmes; collections for the poor, &c. every Lords day. For *Officers* and publique Rulers in the Church, we fet up no other but the very fame which the reformed Churches judge neceffary and fufficient, and as inftituted by Chrift and his Apoftles for the perpetuall government of his Church, that is, *Paftors, Teachers, Ruling Elders,* (with us not lay but Ecclefiaftique perfons feparated to that fervice) and *Deacons.* And for the matter *of governement and cenfures of the Church,* we had nor executed any other but what all acknowknowledge, namely, *Admonition*, and *Excommunication* upon obstinacie and impenitencie, (which we blesse God we never exercised.) This latter we judged should be put in execution, for no other kind of sins then may evidently be presumed to be perpetrated against the parties known light; as whether it be a sin in manners and conversation, such as is committed against the light of nature, or the common received practices of Christianity, professed in all the Churches of Christ; or if in opinions, then such, as are likewise contrary to the received principles of Christianity, and the power of godlinesse, professed by the party himselfe, and universally acknowledged in all the rest of the churches, and no other sins to be the subject of that dreadful sentence.

And for our directions in these or what ever else requisite to the manage of them, we had these three Principles more especially in our eye, to guide and steere our practice by.

First, the supreame rule *without us*, was the Primitive patterne and example of the churches erected by the Apostles. Our consciences were possessed with that reverence and adoration of the fulnesse of the Scriptures, that there is therein a compleat sufficiencie, as to make the *man of God perfect*, so also to make the Churches of God perfect, (meere circumstances we except, or what rules the law of nature doth in common dictate) if the directions and examples therein delivered were fully known and followed. And although we cannot professe that sufficiency of knowledge as to be

C   able

able to lay forth all thofe rules therein which may meet with all cafes and emergencies that may or fometimes did fal out amongft us, or that may give fatisfaction unto all Queres poffible to be put unto us ; yet we found principles enough, not onely *fundamentall* and effential to the being of a Church, but *fuperftructory* alfo for the wel-being of it, and thofe to us cleare and certaine, and fuch as might well ferve to preferve our Churches in peace and from offence, and would comfortably guide us to heaven in a fafe way : And the obfervation of fo many of thofe particulars to be laid forth in the Word, became to us a more certaine evidence and cleare confirmation that there were the like rules and ruled cafes for all occafions whatfoever, if we were able to difcerne them. And for all fuch cafes wherein we faw not a cleare refolution from Scripture, example, or direction, wee ftil profeffedly fufpended, untill God fhould give us further light, not daring to eeke out what was defective in our light in matters Divine with humane prudence, (the fatall errour to Reformation) left by *fowing* any *piece of the old garment* unto *the new,* we fhould make the *rent worfe*; we having this promife of grace for our encouragement in this, which in our publique Affemblies was often for our comfort mentioned, that *in thus doing the will of God we fhould know more.*

A fecond Principle we carryed along with us in all our refolutions, was, Not to make our prefent judgement and practice a binding law unto our felves for the future, which we in like manner made

con-

continuall profeſſion of upon all occaſions. We had too great an inſtance of our own frailty in the former way of our conformity; and therefore in a jealouſie of our ſelves, we kept this reſerve, (which we made open and conſtant profeſſions of) to alter and retract (though not lightly) what ever ſhould be diſcovered to be taken up out of a miſ-underſtanding of the rule: Which Principle wee wiſh were (next to that moſt ſupreame, namely, to be in all things guided by the perfect wil of God) enacted as the moſt *ſacred law* of all other, in the midſt of all other Laws and Canons Eccleſiaſtical in Chriſtian States and Churches throughout the world.

Thirdly, we are able to hold forth this true and juſt Apologie unto the world, That in the matters of greateſt moment and controverſie, we ſtil choſe to practice ſafely, and ſo, as we had reaſon to judge that all ſorts, or the moſt of all the Churches did acknowledge warrantable, although they make *additaments* thereunto.

For inſtance: Whereas one great controverſie of theſe times is about the *qualification of the Members* of Churches, and the promiſcuous receiving and mixture of good and bad; Therein we choſe the better part, and to be ſure, received in none but ſuch as all the Churches in the world would by the balance of the Sanctuary acknowledge faithful. And yet in this we are able to make this true and juſt profeſſion alſo, That the Rules which we gave up our judgements unto, to judge thoſe vve received in amongſt us by, vvere of that latitude

titude

titude as would take in any member of Christ, the
meanest, in whom there may be supposed to be the
least of Christ, and indeed such and no other as all
the godly in this Kingdome carry in their bosomes
to judge others by. We took measure of no mans
holinesse by his opinion, whether concurring with
us, or adverse unto us; And Churches made up
of such, we were sure no Protestant could but approve of, (as touching the members of it) to be a
true Church, with which communion might be
held. Againe, concerning the great ordinance of
Publique Prayer and the *Lyturgie* of the Church,
whereas there is this great controversie upon it a-
bout the lawfulnesse of set formes prescribed; we
practiced (without condemning others) what all
sides doe allow, and themselves doe practice also,
that the publique Prayers in our Assemblies should
be framed by the meditations and study of our own
Ministers, out of their own gifts, (the fruits of
Christs Ascension) as well as their Sermons use to
be. This vve vvere sure all allowed of, though
they superadded the other. So likewise for the government and discipline in the Churches, however
the practice of the Reformed Churches is in greater matters to govern each particular congregation
by a combined *Presbyterie* of the *Elders* of several
congregations united in one for government; yet
so, as in their judgements they allow, especially in
some cases, a particular congregation, an entire
and compleat power of jurisdiction to be exercised
by the Elders thereof within it selfe; Yea and our
own Master *Cartwright*, holy *Baynes*, and other old
Non-

Non-conformifts, place the power of Excommunication in the Elder fhip of each particular Church
with the confent of the Church, untill they do mifcarry, and then indeed they fubject them to fuch
Presbyterial and Provincial Affemblies as the
proper refuge for appeales and for compounding
of differences amongft Churches; which combination of Churches others of them therefore call
Ecclefiæ ortæ, but particular congregations *Ecclefiæ primæ*, as wherein *firftly* the power and priviledg
of a Church is to be exercifed. And vvithall vve
could not but imagine, that the firft Churches plan-
ted by the Apoftles, were ordinarily of no more in
one city at firft then might make up one entire
congregation, ruled by their own Elders, that alfo
preached to them; for that in every city where
they came, the number of converts did or fhould
arife to fuch a multitude as to make feveral and fun-
dry congregations, or that the Apoftles fhould ftay
the fetting up of any Churches at all, until they rofe
to fuch a numerous multiplication as might make
fuch a Presbyterial combination, we did not imagine. We found alfo thofe *Non-conformifts* (that
wrote againft the Epifcopal Government) in their
Anfwer to the Arguments ufed for Epifcopal Government over many Churches, brought from the
inftances of the multitude of Beleevers at *Jerufalem*,
and other places and cities, mentioned in the New
Teftament, to affert that it could not be infallibly
proved that any of thofe vve reade of in the *Acts*
and elfewhere; vvere yet fo numerous, as neceffa-
rily to exceed the limits of one particular congre-

gation

gation in thofe firft times. We found it alfo granted by them all, that there fhould be feveral Elders in every congregation, who had power over
them in the Lord; and we judged that all thofe
precepts, *obey your Elders*, and *them that are over you*,
were (to be fure, and all grant it) meant of the
Paftours and Teachers, and other Elders that were
fet over them in each particular congregation refpectively, and to be as certainly the intendment of
the holy Ghoft, as in thofe like commands, *Wives
obey your owne husbands*, *Servants your own governours*,
to be meant of their feveral Families refpectively.

We could not therefore but judge it a fafe and
an allowed way to retaine the government of our
feverall congregations. for matter of difcipline
within themfelves, to be exercifed by their own
Elders, whereof we had (for the moft part of the
time we were abroad) three at leaft in each congregation, whom we were fubject to: yet not
clayming to our felves an *independent power* in every
congregation, to give account or be fubject to
none others, but onely a ful and entire power compleat within our felves, until we fhould be challenged to erre grofly; fuch as *Corporations* enjoy, who
have the power and priviledge to paffe fentence for
life & death within themfelves, and yet are accountable to the State they live in. But that it fhould
be the inftitution of Chrift or his Apoftles, that the
combination of the Elders of many Churches
fhould be the firft compleat and entire feat of
Church power over each congregation fo combined; or that they could challenge and affume
that

that authority over those Churches they feed and teach not ordinarily by virtue of those fore-mentioned Apostolicall precepts, was to us a question, and judged to be an *additament* unto the other, which therefore rested on those that allowed us what we practised, over and above, to make evident and demonstrate (and certainly of all other the challenge of all spiritual power from Christ had need have a cleare pattent to shew for it) Yea wee appeale further unto them that have read bookes, whether untill those latter wrytings of the two reverend and learned *Divines of Scotland* set forth after our return, nor much more then two yeeres since, and others of no elder date from *Holland*, and one of our *own* Divines more lately written with much learning and ingenuity ; there hath been much settly and directly or with strength insisted on to prove that governement; and although assert and inculcate it they do as their opinions, yet the full strength and streame of our Non-conformists wrytings and others are spent rather in arguments against, & for the overthrowing the Episcopall government , and the corruptions that cleave to our worship, and in maintayning those severall Officers in Churches which Christ hath instituted in stead thereof (in which we fully agree with them) then in the proofe of a combined classicall Presbyteriall government as it is *authoritatively* practised in the most reformed Churches.

And whereas the common prejudice and exception laid into all mens thoughts against us and our opinions is, that in such a congregationall governement

ment thus entire within it felf, there is no allowed
fufficient remedy for mifcarriages, though never fo
groffe; no reliefe for wrongful fentences or perfons injured thereby; no roome for complaints:
no powerful or effectual means to reduce a
Church or Churches that fal into herefie, fchifme,
&c. but every one is left and may take liberty
without controule to do what is good in their own
eyes; we have (through the good providence of
God upon us) from the avowed declarations of
our *judgements* among our Churches mutually during our exile, and that alfo confirmed by the moft
folemne inftance of our *practice*, wherewith to vin-
dicate our felves and way in this particular; which
upon no other occafion we fhould ever have made
thus publique.

God fo ordered it that a fcandall and offence fell
out between thofe very Churches whilft living in
this banifhment (whereof we our felves, that write
thefe things, were then the Minifters) one of our
Churches having unhappily depofed one of their
Minifters, the other judged it not onely as too fud-
daine an act (having proceeded in a matter of fo
great moment without confulting their fifter
Churches, as was publiquely profeffed we fhould
have done in fuch cafes of concernement) but alfo
in the proceedings thereof as too fevere, and not
managed according to the rules laid down in the
word. In this cafe our Churches did mutually
and univerfally acknowledge and fubmit to this as
a facred and undoubted principle and fupreame
law to be obferved among all Churches, that as by
virtue

virtue of that Apoſtolical command , Churches as wel as particular men *are bound to give no offence neither to Iew nor Gentile, nor the Churches of God* they live amongſt. Sothat in all caſes of ſuch offence or difference, by the obligation of the cõmon law of *cõmunion of Churches*, & for the *vindication of the glory of Chriſt*, which in cõmon they hold forth, the church or churches chalenged to *offend* or *differ*, are to ſubmit themſelves (upon the challenge of the offence or complaint of the perſon wronged) to the moſt full & open tryall & examination by other neighbour Churches offended thereat, of what ever hath given the offence: And further, that by the virtue of the ſame and like law of *not partaking in other mens ſins*, the Churches offended may & ought upon the impenitency of thoſe Churches, perſiſting in their errour and miſcarriage to pronounce that heavy ſentence, againſt them , of with-drawing and renouncing all Chriſtian communion with them until they do repent ; And further to declare and proteſt this, with the cauſes thereof, to all other Churches of Chriſt, that they may do the like.

And what further *authority*, or proceedings purely *Eccleſiaſticall*, of one, or many ſiſter Churches towards another whole Church, or Churches offending, either the Scriptures doe hold forth, or can rationally be put in execution (without the Magiſtrates interpoſing a power of another nature, unto which we upon his particular cogniſance, and examination of ſuch cauſes, profeſſe ever to ſubmit, and alſo to be moſt vvilling to have recourſe unto) for our parts vve ſavv not then, nor do yet ſee. And

like-

likewife we did then fuppofe, and doe yet, that this principle of fubmiffion of Churches that mifcarry unto other Churches offended, together with this other, that it is a command from Chrift enjoyned to Churches that are finally offended to denounce fuch a fentence of *Non-communion* and *withdrawing* from them whilft impenitent, as unworthy to hold forth the name of Chrift, (*thefe* principles being received and generally acknowledged by the Churches of Chrift to be a mutuall duty, as ftrictly enjoyned them by Chrift as any other) that thefe would be as effectuall means (through the bleffing of Chrift) to awe and preferve Churches and their Elders in their duties, as that other of claime to an authoritative power Ecclefiaftical to *Excommunicate* other Churches or their Elders offending; For if the one be compared with the other, in a meere Ecclefiaftial notion, *That* of Excommunication pretended hath but this more in it, That it is a *delivering* of whole Churches and their Elders offending *unto Satan*, (for which we know no warrant in the Scriptures, that Churches fhould have fuch a power over other Churches) And then as for the binding obligation both of the one way &the other, it can be fuppofed to lye but in thefe 2. things; Firft, in a warrant and injunction given by Chrift to his Churches, to put either the one or the other into execution; and 2. that mens confciences be accordingly taken therewith, fo as to fubject themfelves whether unto the one way or the other: For fuppofe that other principle of an *authoritative* power in the greater part of Churches com-

combined to excommunicate other Churches, &c.
to be the ordinance of God, yet unleſſe it doe take
hold of mens conſciences, and be received amongſt
all Churches, the offending Churches will ſleight
all ſuch *Excommunications* as much, as they may be
ſuppoſed to doe our way of proteſtation and ſentence of *Non-communion.* On the other ſide, let this
way of ours be but as ſtrongly entertained, as that
which is the way and command of Chriſt, and upon all occaſions be heedfully put in execution, it
will awe mens conſciences as much, and produce
the ſame effects. And if the Magiſtrates power
(to which we give as much, and (as we think)
more, then the principles of the Presbiteriall government will ſuffer them to yeeld) doe but aſſiſt
and back the ſentence of other Churches denoun-
cing this *Non-communion* againſt Churches miſcar-
rying, according to the nature of the crime, as they
judge meet, and as they would the ſentence of
Churches excommunicating other Churches in
ſuch caſes, upon their own particular judgement of
the cauſe; then, without all controverſie this our
way of Church proceeding wil be every way as
effectuall as their other can be ſuppoſed to be; and
we are ſure, more brotherly and more ſuited to that
liberty and equality Chriſt hath endowed his
Churches with. But without the Magiſtrates interpoſing their authority, their way of proceeding
will be as ineffectuall as ours; and more lyable to
contempt, by how much it is pretended to be more
authoritative; and to inflict a more dreadfull puniſh-
ment, which carnall ſpirits are ſeldome ſenſible of.
This for our judgements.   D 2   And

And for a *reall evidence* and *demonstration* both that this was then, our judgements, as likewise for an instance of the effectuall successe of such a course held by Churches in such cases, our own practice, and the blessing of God thereon, may plead and testifie for us to all the world. The manage of this transaction in briefe was this.

That Church which (with others) was most scandalized, did by letters declare their offence, requiring of the Church (supposed to be) offending, *in the name* and for the vindication of the honour of Christ, and the releeving the party wronged, to yeeld a full and publique hearing before all the Churches of our Nation, or any other whomsoever, offended, of what they could give in charge against their proceedings in that deposition of their Minister, and to subject themselves to an open tryall and review of all those forepassed carriages that concerned that particular; which they most cheerfully and readily (according to the fore-mentioned principles) submitted unto, in *a place*, and *state* where no outward violence or any other externall authority either civil or ecclesiasticall would have enforced them thereunto : And accordingly the Ministers of the Church offended with other two Gentlemen, of much worth, wisdom and piety, members thereof, were sent as *Messengers* from that Church; and at the introduction and entrance into that solemne assembly (the solemnity of which hath left as deep an impression upon our hearts of Christs dreadfull presence as ever any we have been present at,) it was openly and publiquely professed

feffed in a fpeech that was the preface to that difcuffion, to this effect, " That it was the moft to be
" abhorred maxime that any Religion hath ever
" made profeffion of, and therefore of all other the
" moft contradictory and difhonourable unto that
" of Chriftianity, that a fingle and particular foci-
" ety of men profeffing the name of Chrift, and
" pretending to be endowed with a power from
" Chrift to judge them that are of the fame body
" and fociety within themfelves, fhould further ar-
" rogate unto themfelves an exemption from
" giving account or being cenfurable by any other,
" either ChriftianMagiftrate above them, or neigh-
" bour Churches about them. So far were our
judgements from that *independent* liberty that is
imputed to us, then, when we had leaft dependency
on this kingdom, or fo much as hopes ever to abide
therein in peace. And for the iffue and fucceffe of
this *agitation*, after there had been for many dayes
as judiciary and full a charge, tryall, and depofition
of witneffes openly afore all commers of all forts,
as can be expected in any Court where Authority
enjoyns it, that Church, which had offended, did as
publiquely acknowledge their finfull aberration
in it, reftored theit *Minifter* to his place again, and
ordered a folemn day of fafting to humble themfelves afore God and men, for their finfull carriage
in it ; and the party alfo which had been depofed
did acknowledge to that Church wherein he had
likewife finned.

Thus we have rendred fome fmal account of thofe,
the faddeft days of our pilgrimage on earth, wherein

although

although we enjoyed God, yet besides many other miseries (the companions of banishment) we lost some friends and companions, our fellow labourers in the Gospel, as precious men as this earth beares any, through the distemper of the place, and our selves came hardly off that service with our healths, yea lives.

When it pleased God to bring us his poor *Exiles* back again in these revolutions of the times, as also of the condition of this kingdom, into our own land, (the pouring forth of manifold prayers and teares for the prosperity whereof, had been no small part of that publique worship we offered up to God in a strange land;) we found the judgement of many of our godly learned brethren in the Ministery (that desired a general reformation) to differ from ours in some things, wherein we do professedly judge the *Calvinian* Reformed Churches of the first reformation from out of Popery, to stand in need of a further reformation themselves; And it may without prejudice to them, or the imputation of Schisme in us from them, be thought, that they comming new out of Popery (as well as *England*) and the founders of that reformation not having *Apostolique infallibility*, might not be fully perfect the first day. Yea and it may hopefully be conceived, that *God* in his secret, yet wise and gratious dispensation, had left *England* more unreformed as touching the outward form, both of worship & Church government, then the neighbour Churches were, having yet powerfully continued a constant conflict and contention

tention for a further Reformation for these foure-
score yeers; during which time he had likewise in
stead thereof blessed them with the spiritual light
(and that encreasing) of the power of Religion in
the Practique part of it, shining brighter and clearer
then in the neighbour Churches, as having in his in-
finite mercy on purpose reserved and *provided some
better thing* for this Nation **when it should** come to
be reformed, that the other Churches might not be
made *perfect without it*, as the Apostle speaks.

We found also (which was as great an affliction
to us as our former troubles and banishment) our
opinions and wayes (wherein we might seem to
differ) environed about with a cloud of mistakes
and misapprehensions, and our persons with re-
proaches, Besides other calumnies, as of *schisme*,
&c. (which yet must either relate to a differing
from the former Ecclesiastical Government of this
Church established, and then who is not involved
in it as well as we? or to that constitution and government that is yet to come; and untill that be
agreed on, established and declared, and actually
exist, there can be no guilt or imputation of Schime
from it) *That* proud and insolent title of *Independencie* was affixed unto us, as our claime; the very
sound of which conveys to all mens apprehensions
the challenge of an exemption of all Churches
from all subjection and dependance, or rather a
trumpet of defiance against what ever *Power, Spirituall* or *Civill*; which we doe abhor and detest: Or
else the odious name of *Brownisme*, together with
all their opinions as they have stated and maintained

ned them, must needs be owned by us: Although upon the very first declaring our judgements in the chief and fundamental point of all *Church discipline,* and likewise since, it hath been acknowledged that we differ much from them. And wee did then, and doe here publiquely professe, we beleeve the truth to lye and consist in a *middle way* betwixt that which is falsly charged on us, *Brownisme*; and that which is the contention of these times, the *authoritative Presbyteriall Government* in all the subordinations and proceedings of it.

And had we been led in our former wayes, and our removall out of this Kingdome by any such *spirit* of *faction* and division, or of *pride* and *singularity,* (which are the usual grounds of all Schisme) we had since our returns again during this intermisticall season, tentations, yea provocations enough to have drawn forth such a spirit; having manifold advantages to make and encrease a partie, which we have not in the least attempted. We found the spirits of the people of this Kingdome that professe or pretend to the power of godlinesse (they finding themselves to be so much at liberty, and new come out of bondage) ready to take any impressions, and to be cast into any mould that hath but the appearance of a stricter way. And we found that many of those mists that had gathered about us, or were rather cast upon our persons in our absence, began by our presence againe, and the blessing of God upon us, in a great measure to scatter and vanish, without speaking a word for our selves or Cause.

But

But through the grace of Christ, our spirits are
and have been so remote from such dispositions &
aymes, that on the contrary we call God and men
towitnes our constant forbearance, either to publish
our opinions by preaching (although we had the
Pulpits free) or to print any thing of our owne or
others for the vindication of our selves (although
the Presses were more free then the Pulpits) or to
act for our selves or way; although we have been
from the first provoked unto all these all sorts of
wayes, both by the common mis-understandings
and mis-representations of our opinions and practises, together with incitements to this State not
to allow us the peaceable practises of our *Consciences*, which the Reformed Churches abroad allowed us, and these edged with calumnies and re-
proaches cast upon our persons in print ; and all
these heightned with this further prejudice and
provocation, that this our silence was interpreted,
that we were either ashamed of our opinions, or a-
ble to say little for them ; when as on the other
side (besides all other advantages) Books have
been written by men of much worth, learning, and
authority, with moderation and strength, to pre-
possesse the peoples minds against what are supposed our Tenets. But we knew and considered that
it was the *second blow that makes the quarrell*, and that
the *beginning of strife* would have been as the *brea-
king in of waters* ; and the sad and conscientious ap-
prehension of the danger of rending and dividing
the godly Protestant party in this Kingdome that
were desirous of Reformation , and of making severall

E

verall interefts among them in a time when there was an abfolute neceffity of their neereft union and conjunction, and all little enough to effect that Reformation intended, and fo long contended for, againft a common adverfary that had both prefent poffeffion to plead for it felfe, power to fupport it, and had enjoyed a long continued fettlement which had rooted it in the hearts of men; And this feconded by the inftant and continuall advices and conjurements of many *Honourable*, wife, and godly *Perfonages* of both *Houfes* of *Parliament*, to forbeare what might any way be like to occafion or augment this unhappy difference; They having alfo by their Declarations to His Majefty profeffed their endeavour and defire to unite the Proteftant partie in this Kingdome, that agree in Fundamentall Truths againft Popery and other Herefies, and to have that refpect to tender confciences as might prevent oppreffions and inconveniences which had formerly been; Together with that ftrict engagement willingly entred into by us for thefe common ends, with the reft of our brethren of the Miniftery, (which though made to continue but *ad placitum*, yet hath been facred to us.) And above all, the due refpect we have had to the peaceable and orderly Reformation of this Church and State; the hopefull expectation we have been entertained with of an happy *latitude* and agreement by means of this *Affembly*, and the wifdome of this *Parliament*: The confcience and confideration of all thefe, and the weight of each, have hitherto had more power with us to this deepe filence and forbearance, then

all

all our own interefts have any way prevailed with us to occafion the leaft difturbance amongft the people. We have and are yet refolved to beare all this with a quiet and a ftrong patience , (in the ftrength of which we now fpeak, or rather figh forth this little) referring the vindication of our perfons to God, and a further experience of us by men; and the declaration of our judgements, and what we conceive to be his truth therein, to the due and orderly agitation of this *Affembly* whereof *both Houfes* were pleafed to make us *Members.*

And whereas our filence upon all the forementioned grounds (for which we know we can never lofe efteeme with good and wife men) hath been by the ill interpretation of fome, imputed either to our confcioufneffe of the badneffe and weakneffe of our Caufe, or to our unability to maintain what we affert in difference from others , or anfwer what hath been written by others, wee fhall (with all modefty) onely prefent this to all mens apprehenfions in confutation of it. That what ever the truth and juftneffe of our Caufe may prove to be, or how flender our abilities to defend it, yet wee pretend at leaft to fo much wifdome, that wee would never have referved our felves for, but rather by all wayes have declined *this Theatre,* of all other, the moft judicious and fevere, an *Affembly* of fo many able, learned, and grave *Divines,* where much of the piety, wifdome, and learning of two Kingdomes are met in one, honoured and affifted with the prefence of the *Worthies* of both *Houfes* at all debates (as often as they pleafe to vouchfafe

E 2   their

their prefence) as the Stage whereon firft wee
would bring forth into publique view our Tenets
(if falfe and counterfet) together with our own
folly and weakneffe: We would much rather have
chofen to have been venting them to the multitude, apt to be feduced, (which we have had thefe
three yeers opportunity to have done.) But in a
confcientious regard had to the orderly and peaceable way of fearching out truths, and reforming the
Churches of Chrift, we have adventured our felves
upon this way of God, wifely affumed by the prudence of the State; And therein alfo upon all forts
of difadvantages (which we could not but forefee)
both of *number*, *abilities* of learning, *Authority*, the
ftreame of *publique intereft*; Trufting God both with
our felves and his own truth, as he fhall be pleafed
to manage it by us.

Moreover, if in all matters of *Doctrine*, we were
not as *Orthodoxe* in our judgements as our brethren
themfelves, we would never have expofed our
felves to this tryall and hazard of difcovery in this
Affembly, the mixture of whofe fpirits, the quick-
fightednes of whofe judgements (intent enough
upon us) and variety of debates about all forts of
controverfies afoot in thefe times of contradiction,
are fuch, as would be fure foon to find us out if we
nourifhed any monfters or Serpents of opinions lurking in our bofomes. And if we had carryed it fo, as that hitherto fuch errours were not
aforehand open to the view and *judgement* of all, yet
fitting here (unleffe we would be filent, which we
have not been) *we could not long be hid.* But it is

fuf-

fufficiently known that in all *points of doctrine*
(which hitherto in the review and examination of
the *Articles* of our Church, or upon other occasions
have been gone thorough) our judgements have
ftill concurred with the greateft part of our brethren, neither do we know wherein we have dif-
fented. And in matters of *Difcipline* (which we
are now upon) when our judgements cannot in all
things concur with others (as indeed not others
all, in all things amongft themfelves) yet we are
fo farre from holding up the differences that occur,
or making the breaches greater or wider, that we
endeavour upon all fuch occafions to grant and
yeeld (as all may fee and cannot but teftifie for us)
to the utmoft latitude of our light and confciences;
profeffing it to be as high a point of Religion and
confcience readily to own, yea fall down before
whatfoever is *truth* in the hands of thofe that differ,
yea though they fhould be enemies unto us, as much
as earneftly to contend for & hold faft thofe truths
wherein we fhould be found diffenting from them;
and this as in relation to peace, fo alfo as a juft due
to truth and goodnes, even to approve it & acknowledge it to the utmoft graine of it, though mingled
with what is oppofite unto us. And further when
matters by difcuffion are brought to the fmalleft
diffent that may be, we have hitherto been found
to be no *backward* urgers unto a temper (not onely in
things that have concerned our own confciences,
but when of others alfo) fuch as may fuit and tend
to union as well as fearching out of truth ; judging
this to be as great and ufefull an end of *Synods*

and

and *Assemblies*, as a curious and exact discussion of all sorts of lesser differences with binding *Determinations* of truth one way.

And thus we have nakedly and with all simplicity rendred a cleare and true account of our wayes and spirits hitherto; Which we made choice of now at first to make our selves known by, rather then by a more exact and *Scholastique* relation of our judgements in the points of difference about *Church government*; reserving that unto the more proper season and opportunity of this *Assembly*, and that liberty given by both Honourable Houses in matters of dissent; or as necessity shall after require, to a more publique way of stating and asserting of them. In the meane time from this briefe historicall relation of our practices, there may a true estimate be taken of our opinions in difference, which being instanced in, and set out by practices, is the most reall and least collusive way, and carries its own evidence with it. All which we have taken the boldnes together with our selves humbly to lay at the feet of *your wisdom and piety*; Beseeching you to look upon us under no other Notion, or character, then as those, who if we cannot assume to have been no way furtherers of that reformation you intend, yet who have been no way hinderers thereof, or disturbers of the publique peace; and who in our judgements about the present work of this age, the reformation of worship and discipline, do differ as little from the Reformed Churches, and our Brethren, yea far lesse, then they do from what themselves were three yeers past, or then the

gene-

generallity of this kingdom from it felf of late. And withall to confider us as thofe, who in thefe former times, for many yeers fuffered even to exile, for what the kingdom it felf now fuffers in the endeavour to caft out; and who in thefe prefent times, and fince the change of them, have endured (that which to our fpirits is no leffe grievous) the oppofition and reproach of good men, even to the threatning of another banifhment, and have been through the grace of God upon us, the fame men in both, in the midft of thefe varieties ; And finally, as thofe that do purfue no other intereft or defigne but a fubfiftance (be it the pooreft and meaneft) in our own land (where we have and may do further fervice, & which is our birth-right as we are men) with the enjoyment of the ordinances of Chrift (which are our portion as we are Chriftians) with the allowance of a latitude to fome leffer differences with peaceablenefle, as not knowing where elfe with fafety, health, and livelyhood, to fet our feet on earth.

Tho: Goodwin, } { *Jer: Burroughes,*
Philip Nye, } {
Sidrach Simpfon } { *William Bridge.*

FINIS.

Notes on the Text

Charles Herle (1598–1659). In 1643 Herle was one of the twelve Divines authorized to license books. He was a graduate of Exeter College, Oxford, and had been associated with the Stanleys (the family of the Earl of Derby). He had also been appointed a representative for Lancashire in the Westminster Assembly. Although he was a Presbyterian he leaned toward conciliation and sometimes we find him acting with the Independents in the Assembly, particularly during the Ordination debate of January 1643/4. The fact that he licensed the *Apologeticall Narration* shows that he thought the Dissenting Brethren had something to say and should be allowed to say it. On the other hand he was firm in his own views. Almost the same time he published a small tract against Independency, *The Independency on Scriptures of the Independency of Churches* (1643), in which the issues presented by Independent church government were " temperately stated." In the Preface to this book Herle declared, " However, for the difference betweene us and our brethren that are for Independency, 'tis nothing so great . . . our difference 'tis such as doth at most but ruffle a little the fringe, not any way rend the garment of Christ, 'tis so farre from being a fundamentall, that 'tis scarce a materiall one, nay not so much as the forme, 'tis but the better or worse way for the exercise of the same forme of discipline that is in question." Perhaps the author made the differences less than they were, but Herle's words emphasize that his temperateness was a most marked quality — he was temperate as between the English and the Scots, and he was temperate as between Independents and Presbyterians. His essential fair-mindedness received recognition when he was appointed Prolocutor of the Westminster Assembly by Parliament on July 22, 1646, after the death of Dr. Twisse. Although he fell under a cloud during the Commonwealth and was under some restraint from 1650–1653, he was apparently allowed to return to his charge at Winwick during Cromwell's Protectorate and remained there until his death in 1659.

Parliament. Parliament was entirely responsible for calling the Westminster Assembly, and the Assembly was on all points accountable to Parliament. Cf. S. W. Carruthers, *The Everyday Work of the Westminster Assembly* (Presbyterian Historical Society, Philadelphia, 1943), chapter II.

M.DCX.LIII, i.e., 1643. The *Apologeticall Narration* actually appeared at the end of January or the beginning of February, 1644, but until 1752 the year changed for dating purposes on March 25. In most modern books, where it is necessary to take into account both styles of dating, it is usual to give dates between January and March in the following way: 1643/4.

PAGE (1)

Heading. " Formerly in Exile." All the signatories to the pamphlet had been exiles in the Netherlands. The probable reasons why the number of those who signed was limited to members of the group who had been exiled in Holland are discussed *infra* pp. 82f., 110ff. See also the note for page (5).

Line 1. " our eares have been. . . ." The whole of this page clearly refers to the obloquy into which the Independent members of the Westminster Assembly had fallen owing to their obstructive tactics in the Assembly. Cf. Robert Baillie, Letter to Scotland, 1st of January, 1643/4, *Letters and Journals* (edited by David Laing, Edinburgh, 1842), II: p. 122.

PAGE (2)

Lines 12–13. " long before some others of our brethren. . . ." See the note referring to page (30).

Line 18 to page (3), line 6. " dark part . . . light part." I.e., the *negative* aspects of the existing church government and liturgy when they went into exile, and the *positive* aspects of church government and liturgy as they believed it to be laid down in the New Testament.

PAGE (3)

Lines 25–26. " We had no new Common-wealths to rear. . . ." To what were the Dissenting Brethren referring? We might be tempted to think that they were referring to the prospect of the English Commonwealth but this is hardly possible. The English Commonwealth did not come into existence until after the King's death and active republicanism had not made its appearance at this early date (although it rapidly gained influence in the army during the last months of 1644, and the following years). But read the quotation above with the accent on " *we*." The most probable reference is to the new Commonwealth which was being established by their brethren and countrymen in New England. I suggest that the Dissenting Brethren were probably answering the gibe that " The Congregational Way " had been formulated to fit in with the new Commonwealth in America — i.e., "*We in Holland* had no

34

new Commonwealth to rear . . ." — this would partly explain why John Phillips was not one of the signatories of the *Apologeticall Narration*. The rest of this page has very clear reference to the " State-ends " of the English and Scot politicians in their struggle with the King.

PAGE (4)

Lines 17–18. " the power of godlinesse and the profession thereof. . . ." The Congregationalists were at one with the Separatists in their insistence that membership in the church implied willingness to walk in the ways of Christ — Christians were to be " visible saints." Cf. G. F. Nuttall, *Visible Saints* (Blackwell, Oxford, 1957), especially chapter 4.

Line 24. " The good old Non-conformists. . . ." N.B. " Non-conformist " has its modern meaning after 1662. The Dissenting Brethren were referring to the Non-conformist members of the Church of England who appeared in the late Tudor and early Stuart periods. In particular they were thinking of those who had refused to conform in the reign of Mary, and those Puritans who had sided with Thomas Cartwright in the reign of Elizabeth. For the incipient forms of Puritanism among the Marian exiles cf. *A Brieff Discours off the Troubles Begonne at Franckford*, attributed to William Whittingham and first published in 1575. [But for the debated question of the authorship of this latter work see " The Authorship of *A Brieff Discours off the Troubles Begonne at Franckford*," by Patrick Collison in *The Journal of Ecclesiastical History*, London, October 1958, Vol. IX, No. 2, pp. 188–208.]

Line 32 to page (5), line 1. " the fatall miscarriages and shipwracks of the Separation. . . ." The history of Separatism in Holland had not been very happy. Insistence upon purity in church life had often lead to censoriousness and hence to division within the churches. Robert Browne, *A True and Short Declaration* (1584), gives an account of the circumstances which caused his quarrel with Robert Harrison and divided the church at Middleburg (*The Writings of Robert Harrison and Robert Browne*, ed. Albert Peel, Leland H. Carlson, Allen and Unwin, London, 1953, pp. 396–429). Similarly, the church at Amsterdam, where Francis Johnson and Henry Ainsworth had settled, had been very bitterly divided.

PAGE (5)

Line 1. " Brownists. . . ." The Separatists very rapidly became known by the name of their most famous apologist, Robert Browne (1550–1633). Cf. Shakespeare's *Twelfth Night* (Act III, Scene 2) " I'd as lief be a Brownist as a politician."

35

Line 18. " into a Wildernes. . . ." The authors refer here to the Puritan migration to Massachusetts. For the extent to which the motives for the migration were economic or religious, cf. Allan French, *Charles I and the Puritan Upheaval* (George Allen and Unwin, London, 1955).

PAGE (6)

Lines 9–11. The Churches and Ministry of the Church of England. The assertion that parochial congregations in the Church of England could be true churches, and that her ministers were true ministers, were fundamental differences between the seventeenth-century " Congregationalists " and the Separatists. It should be remembered that this was one of the main issues between Roger Williams and the Congregational authorities in Massachusetts.

PAGE (7)

Margin. " Mr. Cheynett. . . ." This is obviously a misprint for Cheynell. Francis Cheynell (1608–1665) was a Puritan minister, and a member of the Westminster Assembly. In 1643 he had published his book to which the Dissenting Brethren were obviously referring, *The Rise, Growth and Danger of Socinianisme.* In this book Cheynell wrote, " There are some reverend and learned *Ministers* in this Kingdome, who are commonly called *Independent Ministers,* and these are all put downe for Brownists, if not Anabaptists . . . I will therefore briefly shew that these Ministers are neither Anabaptists nor Brownists." *Ibid.,* p. 65.

Lines 25–26. " the priviledge of ringing a publique bell. . . ." In the Netherlands particularly, where the inhabitants had been constantly subjected to invasion and war, bells assumed a very great importance, for they summoned the soldiers to defend the town as well as summoning Christians to church. For this reason the bell of the cathedral, or chief church in a city, often belonged to the city rather than to the church.

Line 30. " Guiciardine. . . ." This is a somewhat frustrating allusion. Presumably the Apologists were referring to Ludovico Guicciardini (1525–1589), and not to his more famous uncle, the historian, Franscesco Guicciardini. The former had written a firsthand description of the Low Countries, *Descrittione di M. Ludovico Guicciardini patritio Fiorentino, di tutti i peasi bassi, altrimenti detti Germania inferiore* (published in Antwerp in 1567). Although village bells are occasionally mentioned it is not possible to trace the specific reference to which the Apologists were alluding. In 1593, however, Thomas Danett published an " epitome " in English, *The Description of the Low Countreys and provinces thereof, gathered into an epitome out the Historie of L. Guicciardini.* This was almost certainly the work from which the authors of the *Apologeticall Narration* obtained their information. The only copy which I have been able to trace was listed in the British Museum Catalogue, and unfortunately this copy has been lost!

PAGE (8)

Lines 27–29. " Ruling Elders, (with us not lay but Ecclesiastique persons separated to that service). . . ." The Apologists were emphasizing a point of agreement with the Presbyterians. Compare what Cartwright says in his *Replye* (1573), p. 496, " therefore although they were not pastors to preach the Word yet were they no laymen, as they termed them but ecclesiastical persons" ; as cited in D. J. McGinn, *The Admonition Controversy* (Rutgers University Press, New Brunswick, 1949), p. 493.

PAGE (9)

Lines 1–3. Excommunication. N. B. Excommunication was only to be upon " obstinacie and impenitencie " and was actually never exercised by the Dissenting Brethren in Holland. This illustrates the grounds on which excommunication was administered, the care which was used not to invoke it lightly, and the solemnity with which it was regarded.

Line 21f. " Primitive patterne. . . ." They had no doubt that there *was* a primitive pattern in the New Testament and that this was to be followed as closely as possible. To this extent they share in the Restorationism that runs through a great deal of early Protestantism.

PAGE (10)

Lines 30–32. " Not to make . . . future. . . ." The principle is reminiscent of Pastor John Robinson's famous aphorism in his sermon to the departing Pilgrims, " the Lord hath yet more light and truth to break forth from his holy Word." Was this a conscious reflection of Robinson? Dr. G. F. Nuttall reminds us that Peter Heylyn, the royalist biographer of Laud, had declared that to avoid the " severe Discipline " of Presbyterianism and the " Licenciousness " of Brownism, they had " embraced Robinsons Moddel of Church-Government in their Congregations." *(Cyprianus Anglicus* [1668], p. 367; quoted by Nuttall, *Visible Saints,* p. 14.) How far was Heylyn a trustworthy observer at this point? There were three strong reasons why the Dissenting Brethren might have regarded Robinson's views with some favor: (a) the excellent reputation of Robinson in Holland; (b) Robinson did not follow the extreme exclusivity of most Brownists; and (c) almost alone among Separatists congregations, his congregation had been a model of unity. Cf. *infra* p. 64, note 18.

PAGE (12)

Lines 1–3. " the meanest . . . the least of Christ. . . ." Here we see a unique position taken by the Congregationalists over against the Separatists and the Presbyterians in the standards they expected for membership of the church. They seem to interpret the principle in two ways. In one sense the Dissenting Brethren seem to lean more towards the Separatists' rigorous insistence upon the visible marks of regeneration and holiness than they do towards the comprehensiveness of a national Church. But they also push the standards of " saintliness " expected of a church member as far as they can be pushed in the direction of leniency and inclusiveness.

Line 26. " Presbyterie of the Elders. . . ." It should be recognized that the Dissenting Brethren were pressing for the recognition of the congregational *presbytery,* and not the sole power of the local congregation. Over against the pastoral power of its presbyters the covenanted members of a local congregation had the right of consent, and it was only later that a " democratic " ecclesiology began to develop. Cf. Thomas Goodwin's *On the Constitution, Right Order, and Government of the Churches of Christ,* Bk. II, chapters V & VI, *Works,* XI: 74ff.; John Owen, *True Nature of a Gospel Church,* chapter IV, *Works,* XVI: 42ff., although it should be noted that Owen speaks of the church as a " voluntary society " (*Ibid.,* p. 66), and he seems to have emphasized the spiritual power of the people (pp. 68ff.); Norton's *Responsio,* chapter IV (p. 77f.). One of the most important contributions which they had to make to the doctrine of the Church was the integral relationship between the membership and the officers in the ministry of the Church *as a whole:* " in an organised church no act can be valid which is taken by the eldership without the fellowship, nor any by the fellowship without the eldership. The Christian Churches are neither a monarchy, an aristocracy nor a democracy, but a theocracy or, if you will, a Christocracy." Norton, *The Answer* (translated by Douglas Horton, The Belknap Press, Cambridge, Mass., 1958), p. 88.

Line 32. " Master Cartwright. . . ." Thomas Cartwright (1535–1600) was the leader of the Elizabethan Puritans who were opposed to the episcopal form of the Church which had been established. In 1569 he had been elected Lady Margaret Professor of Divinity at Cambridge, but because of his radical anti-episcopal views had been deprived of his chair the following year at the instigation of John Whitgift. He entered into a lengthy literary duel with Whitgift, who became Archbishop of Canterbury in 1583. The Puritans were driven underground, and Cartwright was silenced and twice suffered imprisonment (1585, 1590–92). Cartwright is usually regarded as the father of English Presbyterianism, although A. F. Scott Pearson admits that "Cartwright himself laid weight upon the prerogatives of congregations in the election of their ministers." (*Thomas Cartwright and Elizabethan Puritanism,* C. U. P., Cambridge, 1925, p. 415.) John Cotton also claimed Cartwright as one of those who had inspired the "Congregational Way," for in *The Way of Congregationall Churches Cleared* (1648), p. 27, he declared, "For the matter of the testimony itself, I conceive, the form of Church-government wherein we walk doth not differ in substance from that which Mr. *Cartwright* pleaded for," and later on the same page he claimed Cartwright's authority for their protest against the mixture of good and bad in the parish churches of England, and for their emphasis upon the local congregational eldership. "And in both these," he declared, "we find Mr. Cartwright's footsteps going plainly before us."

Line 32. "holy Baynes. . . ." Paul Baynes (?–1617) after a somewhat dissolute youth had been converted. He became lecturer at St. Andrew's Church, Cambridge, on the death of William Perkins. He was silenced by Dr. Hasnet, Chancellor to Archbishop Bancroft, and was therefore forced into nonconformity. The last part of his life was spent in comparative penury, but he was a welcome guest in the homes of several Puritan gentry. Cf. Paul Baynes's *The Diocesans Tryall* (1621, 1644), pp. 4–23; his *Commentary on Ephesians* had been published in 1643.

PAGE (13)

Lines 9–10. "Ecclesiae ortae . . . Ecclesiae primae. . . ." I.e., *derived* churches *(ecclesiae ortae),* as distinct from *primary* churches *(ecclesiae primae).* They were claiming that the single covenanted church, duly constituted with its officers, was the primary form of the Church from which all other forms of the Church were derived.

Lines 15–16. "ruled by their own Elders, that also preached to them. . . ." Here the essential relationship between church discipline and pastoral care and worship is very clearly implied.

PAGE (15)

Lines 12–16. " two reverend and learned Divines of Scotland . . . learning and ingenuity. . . ." We wish that the Dissenting Brethren had been rather more explicit about the books on Presbyterianism that they had in mind. The works which they mention as coming out of Scotland would most probably be Samuel Rutherford's *A Peaceable and Temperate Plea for Pavl's Presbyterie, or A Modest and Brotherly Dispute of the government of the Church of Scotland, Wherein, etc. the grounds of Separation and the Independencie of particular Congregations, etc. are examined and tried* (1642), and George Gillespie's *The Government of the Church of Scotland in the point of Ruling Elders* (1641). As for those " from Holland," the writers may be referring to John Paget's " Twenty Propositions," which were issued to Thomas Hooker in 1632, and to his *A Defence of Chvrch Government exercised in Presbyteriall, Classical & Synodall Assemblies, according to the practice of the Reformed Churches* (1641). At this date it could *not* be a reference to the work of Apollonius. The conciliatory and somewhat gracious reference to " one of our own Divines " is clearly a reference to the book of their licenser, Charles Herle, who about this time published *The Independency on the Scriptures of the Independency of Churches* (1643) ; cf. Edwards, *Antapologia*, p. 125. Edwards was very put out that the Dissenting Brethren had not seen fit to mention his own book, *Reasons against the Independent Government of Particular Churches; as also against the Toleration of such Churches to be erected in this Kingdome* (1641) ; cf. *Antapologia*, pp. 125, 228, 233.

PAGE (16)

Lines 17–18. " a scandall and offence fell out. . . ." The Dissenting Brethren base a good deal on their dealings in the synod that was called to resolve the difficulties in the congregation at Rotterdam. It should therefore all the more carefully be compared with Thomas Edwards's interpretation of the same incident in his *Antapologia* (1644), pp. 35–38, 142ff.

PAGE (18)

Lines 20–21. " delivering of whole Churches and their Elders offending unto Satan. . . ." Thomas Edwards protested most vigorously against this " scandalous charge," and declared that it was a sentence which " never yet was heard of any in the reformed Churches for the space of a hundred yeares past " ; *Antapologia*, p. 151, cf. *Ibid.*, p. 153.

PAGE (19)

Lines 27–33. The Magistrate's Power. Edwards was particularly incensed with this passage, because he thought it implied that Presbyterianism " does not give Magistrates the ecclesiastical power which is their due " (*op. cit.,* p. 155). He quoted a passage from the Remonstrants and showed how they had cried up the power of the Magistrate against the Synod of Dort, but he prophesied that in the end the Dissenting Brethren would treat Parliament as the Remonstrants had treated the Dutch Estates (*op. cit.,* pp. 155–58). He also showed from a passage out of Burroughes' *Commentary on Hosea* that Burroughes would give the Magistrate no more power " then the rigidest Presbyterians " (*Ibid.,* p. 159).

PAGE (23)

Lines 24–31. " Independencie . . . Brownisme. . . ." Edwards was particularly vitriolic in reply to this passage. On their refusal to be known as Brownists, he declared, " In generall, how ever you doe in words wash your hands of these imputations, and wipe your mouthes, confidently denying them, yet all the water in the Thames will not wash you from all just imputation of these . . ." (*op. cit.,* p. 197, and following). He asks at what point in church discipline did they differ from Browne? (*Ibid.,* p. 206.)

PAGES (24–27)

The Dissenting Brethren claimed that they had not tried to make a party to support them, and that they had assiduously refrained from publishing their views in pulpit or in print. Edwards deals with these claims in detail. He charges them with having taken all possible chances to create a party (*op. cit.,* pp. 210–11), itemizes the sermons they had preached in favor of their way (*Ibid.,* pp. 215–22), and says that they had followed a deliberate policy of obstruction in the Assembly (*Ibid.,* pp. 227, 251, 268f.).

PAGE (26)

Lines 23–24. " which though made to continue ad placitum, yet hath been sacred to us. . . ." I.e., although the agreement not to publish anything that might jeopardize relationships in the Assembly had been made only for the sake of peace, they claim that they have regarded the promise as binding. Edwards, of course, interpreted things very differently. He maintained that Burroughes, Bridge, Simpson and Goodwin had all preached in favor of their views, and although open complaints against them had been lodged, the ' peace ' " was still continued notwithstanding some breach on the Independent side, in reference to the publike union against the common enemy, and for those common ends, which was the first ground of it." *Antapologia,* p. 239, cf. *Ibid.,* pp. 240ff.

PAGE (29)

Line 15. " to the utmost latitude of our light and consciences. . . ." A direct reference to the Protestation which they had taken on entering the Assembly, and which bound each member to maintain only " what I think in my conscience to be truth." Jeremiah Burroughes said in his *Irenicum,* 1646, " we come as farre as we have light to guide us, we dare not step one step in the dark; if we doe we shall certainly sinne." (*Op. cit.,* p. 47.)

PAGE (30)

Line 12f. " that liberty given by both Honourable Houses in matters of dissent. . . ." There was liberty at the moment because no system of church government had been set up to replace the episcopal form. But the whole of this page and the one that follows is really a plea that the existing freedom from restraint will be maintained by Parliament.

Lines 31ff. " yea far lesse, then they do from what themselves were three yeers past. . . ." This was a shrewd blow at those who were now supporters of the Presbyterian system in the Assembly, for as the Dissenting Brethren point out, by far the great majority of ministers had been willing to conform to the episcopal system when it had been in power. On November 30th, 1643, Thomas Bayley had declared in the Westminster Assembly, " that till the last year he had lived convinced by Bishop Bilsen (Bilson) of the ' jus divinum' of bishops; till conferring with a gentlewoman, who said, It is a wonder that you cannot see ground for presbyterial government, which all the reformed churches have, which struck him so, that he (Bayley) fell to study the reformed writers, Calvin, Beza, &c., and by them was convinced." Lightfoot's *Journal* (edited by John R. Pitman, Vol. XIII of Lightfoot's *Works,* London, 1824), p. 67. It is quite clear that the conversion of many other members of the Assembly on church government had been as recent as that of Thomas Bayley.

I

English Independents and New England Puritans

B IG MANIFESTOES often begin as little documents. In July, 1643, the Long Parliament in England convened by Ordinance the Westminster Assembly of Divines, which was entrusted to make recommendations to Parliament for the future settlement of the country. Early the following year there appeared the *Apologeticall Narration,* a brief pamphlet of thirty-one octavo pages written by five of the " Dissenting Brethren " to explain their adherence to the " Congregational Way " and their reasons for dissenting from the Presbyterian views of the majority of their colleagues in the Assembly.[1] The pamphlet was written in reaction to the rumors and veiled calumnies that were current in the country, and which the writers thought were directed mainly against them in the mind of the general populace. It was to that extent not a systematic statement of their position, but a personal *apologia.* It was, however, written by men who, saving only in their doctrine of the Church, considered themselves to be as orthodox in their Calvinism as any others in the Assembly, and who if they dissented at this point did so for the sake of the same Scriptural principle of authority which John Calvin had persuaded them to accept in matters religious.

---

[1] For the date of the *Apologeticall Narration* see David Masson, *The Life of John Milton* (Macmillan, London, 1873), III: 23f., Williston Walker, *The Creeds and Platforms of Congregationalism* (Charles Scribner's Sons, New York, 1893; new edition published by The Pilgrim Press, Boston, 1960), p. 137. On February 18th, 1643/4, Robert Baillie, one of the Scottish Commissioners, wrote to Mr. William Spang at Veere in Holland and mentioned that the *Apologeticall Narration* had appeared. [*Letters and Journals of Robert Baillie A.M.* (Edinburgh, 1841, edited by David Laing), II: 129f.] It seems certain that the pamphlet became public at the end of January 1643/4, or very early in February. See the note on the date *supra* in the " Notes on the Text," p. 34.

Although those nominated to the Assembly were all " orthodox " in their adherence to the main tenets of Calvinistic theology, it appears to have been recognized from the first that there were four main schools of thought among them regarding their understanding of the Church.[2] It was perhaps to be expected that, recruited as it was mainly from Parliament's Puritan supporters, the majority would favor the Presbyterian system of Calvin and his continental followers, and that they would regard this system as *de jure divino*. But a number of moderate Episcopalians had also been invited, Dr. James Ussher, the Archbishop of Armagh, Dr. Samuel Ward, Lady Margaret Professor of Divinity at Cambridge and Master of Sidney Sussex College, Dr. Daniel Featley, and Robert Saunderson, who was later to be the bishop of Lincoln. However, out of deference to the King's command, none of the Episcopal party — with the single exception of Dr. Daniel Featley, who was soon removed[3] — took part in the Assembly. To whatever extent they were prepared to debate the episcopal system *de jure divino,* they all certainly supported it as *de jure regis.* The third party was represented by the Erastians who questioned the whole conception of a divine order for the Church, and regarded the State as having the right to fix Church order as it pleased. This party included several of the politicians in the Assembly such as Bulstrode Whitelocke, and scholars such as John Selden, Dr. John Lightfoot and Thomas Coleman.[4] The Solicitor, Oliver St. John,

---

[2] Daniel Neal, *History of the Puritans,* II : 264ff. (originally published in 1732–38). The references are to the 3 volume edition published by Thomas Tegg & Son, London, 1837. Cf. also Thomas Fuller, *The Church History of Britain* (1655), Bk. XI, Section V, #2. References are to the London edition of 1837, edited by James Nichols and published by Thomas Tegg & Son, Vol. III, p. 466f.

[3] Dr. Featley was expelled from the Assembly, and his livings sequestered; for his correspondence with Archbishop Ussher about the affairs of the Assembly cf. Clarendon's *History of the Rebellion,* VII: 254f. [Bishop Warburton's edition, Oxford, 1849, III: 213f.] Philip Nye obtained Featley's living at Acton, Middlesex, and John White (formerly of Dorchester) the rectory of Lambeth. Cf. *infra* p. 92 and note.

[4] Daniel Neal points out that the Erastian position was the view virtually taken by the early English reformers and bishops (e.g., Cranmer, Whitgift), who argued for the supremacy of the Crown in ecclesiastical matters. *Op. cit.,* p. 265. Neal cites Whitgift against Thomas Cartwright. We might add the testimony

was sometimes numbered with this group, although he was equally active in the House of Commons on behalf of the Independents.

The Independents (or Congregationalists) were the fourth party, and in view of the voluntary absence of the Episcopalians and the preoccupation of the Erastians with the relationship between the State and the Church, the most important issues in pure ecclesiology were those which centered in the debate between the Independent minority and the Presbyterian majority in the Assembly. For this reason the *Apologeticall Narration* initiated a period of intense intellectual activity about the nature of the Church which produced most of the great classics in the Congregational understanding of that doctrine.

One particular that emerges from a study of the paper war which followed the appearance of the *Apologeticall Narration* has been curiously under-emphasized on both sides of the Atlantic by historians writing a few years ago.[5] It is the fact that the Dissenting Brethren of the Westminister Assembly and the Puritan church leaders in New England represented one and the same movement in the history of the Church. A seventeenth-century church historian like Thomas Fuller found no difficulty at all in seeing the identity. " Such as desire further instruction in the tenets of these Congregationalists," he said, " may have recourse to those pamphlets written *pro* and *con* thereof. . . . Only I will add that, for the main, the churches of New England are the same in discipline with these Dissenting Brethren."[6]

---

of Richard Bancroft, "the Church of Christ can alwayes content her self with the manner and forme of governement wch the place or Contrye requireth where she is established, and to affirme the contrarie is Anabaptisticall. . . . If anye one certeyne platforme had bene prescribed, wch onelye ought to haue bene followed vppon all occasions, at all tymes, and in all places, no doubt the Apostles would evermore haue vsed it: But the Apostles . . . vsed not any one order or mann^r of governm^t, but altered ye same as occasion required: Therfore there is no one Platforme sett downe to be always followed." *Tracts ascribed to Richard Bancroft,* edited by Albert Peel (Cambridge University Press, Cambridge, 1949), p. 107f.

[5] Professor Perry Miller is a notable exception in his *Orthodoxy in Massachusetts* (Harvard University Press, Cambridge, Mass., 1933). But see the note *infra* p. 52, note 26.

[6] *The Church History of Britain* (1837 edition), III: 467.

It may not be regarded as too palatable a fact in either England or America, but we must remember that the Puritan founders of the New England States regarded themselves, and were regarded by their colleagues at home, simply as transplanted Englishmen! The New England divines were respected by the new leaders in English affairs for the part they had played before their emigration, and the Puritan leaders of the Congregational Way in the homeland looked to them to provide the theological and experimental defense of Congregational polity that would enable their representatives in the Assembly to make a respectable showing : New England alone could provide an authoritative answer to the question " how do you know that it will work? " However, the influence of this intellectual ferment about the doctrine and polity of the Church was no one-way affair. The debate was to swing backwards and forwards across the Atlantic through persons and books for more than a century, and in this process the Congregationalists of both England and America hammered out their understanding of the doctrine and the Scriptural pattern of the Church's polity. Whether they were called " Independents "[7] in England (a term which they abhorred and repudiated) or Puritans in New England, they were part of the same movement in English Puritanism which adhered to a thoroughly Congregational view of the Church, and which opposed with equal vigor the claims of episcopal prelacy and the charge of Brownist Separatism. Now, by the intransigence of their Presbyterian colleagues insisting on complete uniformity in doctrine, polity and

---

[7] The difficulty with the term " Independent " in seventeenth-century England is that it was often used as an inclusive term to describe all those who were neither supporters of the King nor supporters of Presbyterian uniformity. It therefore had both a political and an ecclesiastical significance. In the former sense it came to represent not only the Dissenting Brethren and those members of Parliament who accepted the Congregational and Non-Separatist view of the Church, but also all those who allied themselves to this party in Parliament for the sake of winning liberty of conscience. For this reason even the ecclesiastical significance of the term was to include not only the Puritans of Congregational sympathies, but Baptists and Separatists of all kinds including the many exotic sects that were springing up in the unsettled state of the country. Naturally, the Presbyterian party (which also had its political aspect, as we shall see) was none too scrupulous about tarring the Dissenting Brethren with the Separatist brush or worse.

worship, they were forced to set themselves equally against Presbyterian claims, and if the force of this threat was felt a little less strongly on the banks of the Connecticut River than it was on the banks of the English Thames, it was nevertheless understood in both places. Whatever the eventual differences, in 1643 the Dissenting Brethren of the Assembly and the New England Puritans represented geographical wings of what was essentially *one* movement: they all revered the Calvinist tradition, they had all received insight from the "old non-conformists," William Perkins, Paul Baynes and particularly William Ames, many of them had been colleagues under the proscription of English episcopacy and amid the difficulties of exile in Holland, and they had all accepted the Scriptural primacy of "the Congregational Way."

The Presbyterians in the Assembly, and particularly the Scots Commissioners were not slow in countering what they regarded as "the errors of that very willfull and obstinate party "[8] and Robert Baillie, in particular, was assiduous in trying to get the European presbyteries and synods to declare their detestation of the Independent position, even to the point of suggesting to his cousin, William Spang of Veere in the Netherlands, what they should say and how they should say it.[9] As we know, the Scots Commissioners were successful in enlisting the support of several "Classes" in Europe,[10] and William Spang stimulated his friend, William Apollonius, of the Dutch Church in Middleburg, to address a series of pertinent questions to the writers of the *Apologeticall Narration* and to publish a book under the authority of the Classis of Walcheren in which he challenged the Independents to set their views down clearly in

---

[8] Letter to Mr. Dickson, September 16th, 1644, *Letters and Journals*, II : 232.

[9] See particularly his letter to Spang, 7th December 1643, *Ibid.,* II : 115, but cf. also *Ibid.,* II : 165, 168, 170, 197, and the letters to David Buchanan, II : 179f., 252, 253f.

[10] The relationship between the divines of the Westminster Assembly and various foreign churches is set out by Dr. S. W. Carruthers in *The Everyday Work of the Westminster Assembly* (Presbyterian Historical Societies of America and England, Philadelphia, 1943), pp. 36–43. But see also Robert Baillie's account of how the letters from the continental churches were received, *op. cit.,* II : 143f., 164f., 202, 239.

writing.[11] The Dissenting Brethren were unwilling to do this too hurriedly. Not only was the political and military situation such that their best hope of success lay in preventing too early a decision in the Assembly, but none of them could claim to know how their system of church government would work in alliance with the State. This evidence could be obtained only from New England, and hence they were forced, not altogether against their will — for the slowness of the Atlantic post might prove a useful ally — to appeal to the ability, erudition and above all *experience* of their friends in Massachusetts and Connecticut.

Therefore it is not surprising that the immediate literary effect of the discussions in Westminster appeared in America. Here the Congregational experiment was still within its first generation,[12] but

---

[11] *Consideratio qvarvndam controversiarum, ad regimen ecclesiae Dei spectantium, quæ in Angliæ regno hodie agitantur, ex Mandato & Jussu Classis Walachrianæ Conscripta* (1644). This was published in English in 1645 as *A Consideration of Certaine Controversies at this time agitated in the Kingdome of England, concerning the Government of the Church of God. Written at the command and appointment of the Walachrian Classis by G. A.* Obviously, Baillie and his friends lost no time in getting the Latin form translated so that it might have the widest possible circulation in Britain, but although Apollonius appears to have been the sole author, the fact which made it of particular value to the Presbyterians was that it bore on its title page the authority of a Dutch classis. An excellent brief account of the intervention of Apollonius into the English dispute is in Dr. Douglas Horton's Introduction to John Norton's *Answer* (translated by Dr. Horton and published by The Belknap Press, Cambridge, Mass., 1958). One could also refer to Baillie's comments to Spang. He welcomed the questions sent by Apollonius (*op. cit.*, II: 180f., 183), but continues to press his cousin to see that the promised book is forthcoming (*Ibid.*, II: 245f.) — indeed it is clear that Apollonius was the one bright star of hope within what Baillie regarded as the general darkness of Europe's theologians. But as soon as the Independents were successful in winning the promise of toleration from Parliament, Baillie was just as ready with the suggestion that Apollonius should turn his attention to the next major threat to the Scots' program in the Assembly, the Erastians (*Ibid.*, II: 265, 365, 371).

[12] Whatever the ultimate influence of the Plymouth Colony on the pattern of American Congregationalism, we must exclude it at this point because the churches of that colony had been born out of the " semi-Separatist " congregation of John Robinson that had first emigrated to Leyden. Of the relationship between the Puritan Congregationalists and the Brownist Separatists in producing the ultimate form of Congregationalism there is a good deal more

it had the advantage of unrestricted control of the territories where it had settled. The debate produced authoritative statements on the Congregational discipline and polity from John Cotton of Boston[13] (whom Baillie had expected would answer Apollonius)[14] and Thomas Hooker of Hartford,[15] while John Norton of Ipswich in Massachusetts was deputed to write the authoritative Latin reply to Apollonius's questions which appeared in 1648.[16] These works, together with those from the pens of other New England ministers,[17] represented a very large consensus on the pattern of New England Congregationalism which was to become systematically embodied by John Cotton and his friends in the Cambridge Platform of 1648.

---

to say, but in repudiating Brownism the writers of the *Apologeticall Narration* show themselves to be very definitely allied to the Puritanism of the Massachusetts Bay leaders. For all practical purposes the commencement of the Bay colony may be dated from 1630.

[13] *The Keyes of the Kingdom of Heaven* (1644), *The Way of the Churches of Christ in New England* (1645), *The Way of the Congregational Churches Cleared* (1648). It should be pointed out that Cotton had already written shorter pieces on Church government, including *The True Constitution of a Particular Church* in 1642.

[14] *Op. cit.*, II: 190. Baillie was very disturbed to learn that Gisbertus Voetius of whom he had had great hopes had approved Cotton's *Keyes of the Kingdom* as " consonant to truth, and the discipline of Holland." *Ibid.*, p. 240.

[15] *A Survey of the Summe of Church Discipline* (1648).

[16] *Responsio ad Totam Quaestionum Syllogen a clarissimo Viro Dom. Guilielmo Apollonio, Ecclesiae Middleburgensis Pastore, propositam*, translated by Douglas Horton as *The Answer* (1958), with the details as given in note 11 p. 48.

[17] Examples which may be cited are Richard Mather's *Church-Government and Church-Covenant Discvssed* (1643), (with William Thompson) *A Modest & Brotherly Answer To Mr. Charles Herle his Book, against the Independency of Churches, etc.* (1644), *A Reply to Mr. Rutherford, or, A Defence of the Answer to Mr. Herles Booke, etc.* (1647) ; Thomas Welde's *An Answer to W. R. his narration of the opinions and practices of the Churches lately erected in New-England* (1644), *A Brief Narration of the Practices of the Churches of New England* (1645) ; Thomas Shepard's *New Englands Lamentation for Old Englands present errours and divisions, etc.*, (with Thomas Allin) *A Defence of the Answer, etc.* (1645).

However, although the literary first-fruits of the Westminister Assembly and the *Apologeticall Narration* came from America, the appearance of the latter and the discussion it engendered was no less significant and determinative for Congregationalism in England itself. At first the Dissenting Brethren seem deliberately to have refrained from launching into print on any hasty or ill-considered defense of their doctrine of the Church, preferring to wait for the more complete and carefully compiled apologia that would come from New England. We must not forget that these men were actively engaged in London during the dark days of a bitterly fought civil war. Apart from all other considerations, of which there were a good number, they did not have the circumstances that made for relaxed and unhurried writing. Nevertheless, in face of the virulence of Thomas Edwards's *Antapologia*[18] and the two parts of his *Gangraena,*[19] in which he charges them with every heresy ancient and modern that is to be found in the book, they were forced to defend themselves. Sidrach Simpson wrote *The Anatomist Anatomis'd* (1644), a brief riposte of a dozen pages to *An Anatomy of Independencie* that had been published against the *Apologeticall Narration* earlier that year,[20] but the mantle of defense against the Presbyterian Edwards seems to have fallen upon Jeremiah Burroughes.

Burroughes's intention, we must remember, was not to present a systematic account of church polity but first, to defend himself and his friends against Thomas Edwards's attack, and then to try and

---

[18] 1644. The full title is, *Antapologia: or, A Full Answer to the Apologeticall Narration of Mr Goodwin, Mr Nye, Mr Sympson, Mr Burroughs, Mr Bridge, Members of the Assembly Divines.* Thomas Edwards was one of the most implacable enemies of Independency in any form, and he was particularly opposed to the principle of toleration in matters of religion. As early as 1641 he had published *Reasons against the Independent Government of particular Congregations: as also against the Toleration of such Churches to be erected in this Kingdome,* which shows that even at that comparatively early date in the war Independency and Toleration were equated in his mind.

[19] *Gangraena: or a Catalogue and Discovery of many of the Errours, Heresies, Blasphemies and pernicious Practises of the Sectaries of this time, vented and acted in England in these four last years* (1646).

[20] Alexander Forbes, *An Anatomy of Independencie, or, a Briefe Commentary, and Moderate Discourse upon the Apologeticall Narration* (1644).

foster a more charitable frame of mind in Presbyterian opposition by emphasizing the extent to which Presbyterians and Congregationalists were in complete accord.[21] He tried to fulfill these intentions in his *Vindication*[22] (1644) and in *Irenicum, to the Lovers of Truth and Peace,* published in the year of his death, 1646. However, although these books were not intended to present the theological case for Non-Separatist Congregationalism, there is enough in them to bring many of the issues into clear focus and to illustrate the closeness of Burroughes's view of the church to that of churches in New England.

But there are also suggestions of tensions that might arise in the future. If we recognize in the *Apologeticall Narration* the same basic view of the Church as that which was professed in New England, we also recognize that in applying that concept within their own situation differences of emphasis and interpretation were likely to develop between the English and American wings of the movement. Professor Perry Miller was the first modern historian to make these differences clear and to recognize how they arose,[23] but what was happening was apparently quite clear to contemporaries in the seventeenth century. " Among themselves," wrote Robert Baillie of the Congregationalists, " there are sundry differences, which time will bring out. They [presumably, those of New England] professe to differ from these of England; but who

---

[21] He even emphasized a similarity about which most of his colleagues in England had had second thoughts, for he maintained that like the Presbyterians, they " who are for a Congregationall way, doe not hold absolute liberty for all religions." (*Irenicum,* p. 41.) Cromwell and many in the Army were moving to the point where they would have ranged themselves against Burroughes here. On the other hand, when Burroughes goes on to explain that " the onely way the Church hath to keep downe errors or heresies is spiritual " he really indicates the different concept of authority between the Presbyterian system and that which he owned. He may also indicate the point at which Congregationalists in England and in New England were likely to grow apart. *Ibid.,* pp. 29–58.

[22] *A Vindication of Mr. Burroughs, Against Mr. Edwards his foule Aspersions in his spreading Gangraena, and his angry Antiapologia. Concluding with a briefe Declaration what the Independents would have.*

[23] *Orthodoxy in Massachusetts, 1630–1650* (Harvard University Press, Cambridge, Mass., 1933), pp. 263–313 *passim.*

knows wherein? The maine seems to be in libertie of conscience."
He went on to point out that both wings of the movement "avow
the divine right of Synods for consulting . . . only they in New
England are more strict and rigid than we, or any Church, to sup-
presse, by the power of the magistrate, all who are not of their
way."[24] In a previous letter, also to his cousin, he had protested
that there was "in all New England, no libertie of living for a
Presbyterian."[25] If John Cotton and his fellow ministers regarded
the Dissenting Brethren's plea for liberty of conscience as an embarrassment to the pure Commonwealth they were trying to establish, this was nothing to the embarrassment which they caused the
Brethren in the Assembly by their own determined refusal to toler-
ate any in the colonies who differed from their view of the Church.

We have to see these differences, however, within their own geographical and political contexts. It remains essentially one movement.[26] It has been pointed out that the New England Puritans had

---

[24] To Spang, May 17th, 1644, *Letters and Journals*, II: 183. Cf. also the quotation from Katherine Chidley's *The Justification of the Independant Chvrches
of Christ* (1641), pp. 34–35, in Miller, *op. cit.*, 278f.

[25] April 19th, 1644, *Ibid.*, II: 168.

[26] Here, while agreeing with Perry Miller's main thesis, I question some of his
emphases. (1) We cannot deny that the Congregationalists in England and
New England grew apart on the issue of toleration during the time of the
English Civil war. But when Dr. Miller suggests that the New England
divines turned to the English Independents only *after* they had been rebuffed
by the Presbyterians, he surely does less than justice to the essential unity of
the two Congregational groups. (*Op. cit.*, p. 277.) They had from the first been
bound together by personal friendship *and* a view of the church that was
practically identical. It makes more sense of the history if we recognize that
they represent one "Congregational" movement working for similar ends in
England and America, and if the English began to differ from their New
England colleagues, the reasons are to be sought within their own special
political situation. Indeed, Dr. Miller seems to concede this when he remarks
that the Independents began as "advocates of Congregationalism" but were
swept on to a new position on the matter of toleration. (*Ibid.*, pp. 270–72.)
(2) Even this statement, however, needs to be refined, for what right have we to
assume that the New England attitude represented authentic Congregationalism
any more than the "new" position of the Apologists? The shift took place, and
undoubtedly the New England divines represented Congregationalism's first
thoughts on the toleration issue; but what was most true to the best insights of
the "Congregational Way"? We could argue just as validly that as events

not had the advantage of being purged by the refining fire of a civil war. They had arrived in the 1630's and their ideas were those of the 1630's, particularly the belief which is specifically to be traced to the Treaty of Augsburg (1555) but which was actually a legacy from the Middle Ages.[27] They believed that the civil magistrate had the right and duty to determine, establish and maintain (by force if necessary) the Church of his choice, and when they arrived in New England they acted in accordance with these beliefs of their time, with which they had grown up and which they had unquestioningly accepted. If they were now in a position where they could control the Magistracy in the land where they had settled, they thought they had a perfect right to purge these territories of any ecclesiastical rivals. In this they were no more and no less than men of their own time.[28]

Those who returned to England from Holland on the outbreak of the struggle between Charles I and his Parliament faced a very different situation. Whatever sanguine hopes they may have entertained about persuading Parliament to go their way, they discovered that in the England of the 1640's they represented but a tiny

---

freed the Dissenting Brethren from out-worn Medieval concepts, they were better able to realize that liberty of conscience was a logical inference from that Biblical view of the Church which Dr. Miller shows us was at the heart of the Congregational position. (Cf. *Ibid.*, pp. 222–27.)

[27] The principle of " Cuius regio, eius religio " which was the justification for the Act of Uniformity of the Elizabethan Settlement.

[28] As a point of ecumenical interest, it is not sufficiently recognized that the organization of national churches backed by the coercive power of the State has been in a major way responsible for perpetuating the divided state of the Church, because once the schisms occurred they were ossified within different cultural settings. Roman Catholic countries, of course, maintained the establishment of Roman Catholicism, but to them were added Lutheran states, Reformed states, Anglican states (in England, Wales and the southern American colonies), and Congregational states (in the New England colonies). An alliance of Church and State which held that it was perfectly proper for the dominant ecclesiastical system to stamp out all rivals produced the illusion of a spurious *national* unity. This obscured to all but the informed and perceptive ecumenical enthusiasts, like Dury and Comenius, the fact that *internationally* the Church was almost irredeemably divided. Toleration may have fostered the appearance of many small sects (although not many survived), but it at least made the situation more flexible and showed the division of the Church for what it was.

53

minority within the Puritan movement, and their position was all the more tenuous because of the political situation that made the English Parliament dependent upon the military assistance of the Scots. They were soon forced to realize that they could continue to exist in England only if Parliament gave formal recognition to the principle of religious toleration.

However, the logic of their own position meant that they could not claim this for themselves if they were not willing to grant it to others, and as it became more and more clear that the Presbyterians, aided and abetted by the Scots, had every intention of establishing Presbyterian uniformity in England, the " Independents " increasingly became the religious and political nucleus around which Separatists, Baptists and a host of sectaries gathered in political and military alliance. As Cromwell later remarked, religious liberty was not the first thing for which they had fought, but Providence finally brought it to that issue so that " at last it proved to be that which was most dear to us."[29] It was the only possible policy to adopt, as the career of those who returned from New England to engage in the Civil War — men like Sir Harry Vane and Hugh Peter — makes very plain; and to do the English Independents credit, when they came to power through the amazing success of Cromwell's arms they did not reverse their policy. That which may have begun as expedient was retained as principle.[30]

---

[29] Speech to Parliament, 22nd January, 1654, *The Writings and Speeches of Oliver Cromwell* (Harvard University Press, Cambridge, Mass., 1937–47), edited by W. C. Abbott, III: 586.

[30] This statement may need some justification in the eyes of those who insist on lumping all Puritans together in responsibility for the rigid imposition of the Directory of Public Worship, and in the eyes of those who ignore the political reasons for the proscription of Anglicanism during the Interregnum. Episcopacy was virtually pledged to the re-establishment of the monarchy. On the other hand, within those constitutional Acts for which the Independents took some responsibility (*The Instrument of Government* of 1653, and [to some extent] *The Humble Petition and Advice* of 1657), there were no *theological* reasons why Anglicans (and even Roman Catholics) might not be tolerated as soon as they ceased to be a political threat. Indeed, Cromwell's conversations with Archbishop Ussher early in 1656 indicate that it was a possibility then, and that toleration for the Anglicans might be expected as soon as the danger of political assassination and insurrection had been removed. For the general question of religious toleration under Cromwell see *The Lord Protector*, pp. 324–33.

Nevertheless, it represents a difference of emphasis as it was to develop in the Congregationalism of England and America, for the English Independents' concern for toleration once more became existentially their own when the Restoration of the monarchy in 1660 forced them into nonconformity, just as the ecclesiastical leaders in New England became more determined to maintain the purity of the Puritan theocracy. It may also have stimulated other differences, for Robert Baillie had observed that the " brethren of New England inclynes more to Synods and Presbyteries, driven thereto by the manifold late heresies, schisms, and factions, broken out among them."[31] The later development of consociations in Connecticut lends some support for the view that the trend in America would be towards a more " presbyterian " form of Congregationalism, whereas in the nonconformist situation after 1660 in which synods and presbyteries found it virtually impossible to function, English Congregationalism would almost inevitably have to concentrate upon the discipline of the local and now (perforce) independent church. In these circumstances, even English Presbyterianism tended to become more " congregational."[32]

The starting point for these trends in Congregationalism was in the debates of the Westminster Assembly and the publication of the *Apologeticall Narration,* and if in New England the line of thought stretches through the writings of Cotton, Hooker and Norton to the *Cambridge Platform* of 1648 and the later *Saybrook Platform* of 1708, in England it reaches just as surely through the writings of Burroughes to those of Thomas Goodwin[33] and John Owen[34] and so on to the *Savoy Declaration* of 1658 and the *Heads of*

---

[31] *Letters and Journals,* II : 146.

[32] Cf. *infra* pp. 56, note 35 ; p. 69, note 2.

[33] Although Goodwin appears to have published nothing during the Assembly, he later wrote a lengthy work on Church government, *On the Constitution, Right, Order, and Government of the Churches of Christ,* which appears as Vol. XI of the 1865 edition of his *Works* (James Nichol, Edinburgh).

[34] *The True Nature of a Gospel Church* (1689), which appears as Vol. XVI in the 1853 edition of his *Works* (edited by William H. Goold, Johnstone & Hunter, Edinburgh). John Owen, who eventually became the Vice-Chancellor of Oxford University and the principal architect of the ecclesiastical settlement of the Protectorate, confessed that he was converted from Presbyterian-

Agreement of 1691.[35] The main lines in the future Anglo-Saxon developments of the Congregational Way were all implicit in the *Apologeticall Narration,* in the circumstances that gave it birth, and in the reactions stimulated by its appearance.

---

ism to Congregationalism by reading John Cotton's *Keyes of the Kingdom* (cf. *A Vindication of the Treatise on the True Nature of Schism* [1657] in his *Works,* XIII: 223f.; cf. Cotton Mather's *Magnalia,* V). Owen eventually became perhaps the greatest systematic theologian of English Puritanism. See *infra* p. 84, note 14.

[35] Williston Walker says that the greatest influence in the *Heads of Agreement* (the ill-fated "paper union" between the English Presbyterians and the Independents in 1691) was that of the New England minister, Increase Mather, who was at that time acting as agent for the Massachusetts Colony in London. Walker pointed out that in this document there is "no implication that church courts, synods, or general assemblies are desirable." (*The Creeds and Platforms of Congregationalism,* p. 447.) However, it is doubtful whether one should make too much apologetic capital out of that fact. In post-Restoration England the failure to mention synods and the like was probably as much due to the practical impossibility of maintaining such assemblies as to any change of view on the part of seventeenth-century Puritans. Even English Presbyterians during this period were forced into something very like Independency. Note, however, the influence of the *Heads of Agreement* upon the American scene. *Ibid.,* p. 448f.

II

"The Congregational Way"

W_{E MUST} try to put the *Apologeticall Narration* within its proper context in the ecclesiological discussion, for if it stands at the beginning of a literary movement in which Congregationalism would have to define itself more precisely, this is only because Congregationalism (albeit not under that name) had already made itself manifest as a rival interpretation of the Church to the others that were in the field. Whatever the influences that brought it into being, and whatever the forms that it might ultimately adopt vis-à-vis Episcopacy and Presbyterianism, already in the minds of some it was a live option to these polities, not as a Separatist movement, but as the future pattern of the Church of England.

The Puritans of Elizabeth's reign — "the good old Non-conformists" — no less than the Separatists, had been entirely concerned with defining their position against Roman Catholicism, and more explicitly against the vestiges of that system which in their view persisted within the Church of the Elizabethan Settlement. There was increasing pressure upon them from the Court in the 1620's and 30's,[1] and therefore their apologetic continued to be

---

[1] The maneuvers of the Puritans in the face of this pressure is of some interest. After the failure of the Hampton Court Conference in 1603, pressure on the Puritans was maintained first by the vigilance of Bancroft (Bishop of London 1597, Archbishop of Canterbury 1604–10), and there was immediately a strong move to put into operation the canons respecting ceremonial and dress. This drove into exile not only Separatists like Ainsworth, Robinson and Smyth, but also some of the more radical non-separatist Puritans like Henry Jacob. The pressure became noticeably stronger again about the year 1620, and it should be noted that in the following year William Laud was presented to his first see (St. Davids). Perhaps they first set their hopes in Virginia. When the Pilgrims had set sail in 1619 they had intended to settle in the northern parts of Virginia, possibly because of the known Puritan sympathies of Sir Edwin Sandys, the Treasurer of the Virginia Company in London. The fact that they

aimed mainly against the diocesan episcopacy. This main direction of their attack continued throughout James I's reign and almost up to the time when the Westminster Assembly was called, but the 1630's were not without hints of new elements which would radically affect the ecclesiastical issue. As the pressure to conform increased during James I's reign, Puritans as well as Separatists went into voluntary exile and found a haven of refuge among the Reformed Churches of the Netherlands. Once free from the tutelage of the King and his bishops they allowed their minds to range freely over the nature of the Church, and were the more ready not only to bring the established church government in England to the

---

settled further north was providential, for in 1624 the Virginia colony was dissolved and the colony brought directly under royal (i.e., Anglican) surveillance. This does not mean that Virginia was founded for specifically Puritan purposes as were the later New England colonies, but the influence was strong. Alexander Whitaker, the first country parson of Virginia and minister of Henrice, in 1614 complained " that so few of our English Ministers, that were so hot against the surplice and subscription come hether, where neither is spoken of." [Cf. *Narratives of Early Virginia 1606–1625* (Barnes & Noble, 1959 edition, edited by Lyon Gardiner Tyler), p. 317. See also *Ibid.,* pp. 272–73 for the laws of the Virginia Assembly governing excommunication. It was after the death of Lord de la Warr, the Governor, in 1619, that the Puritan Sir Edwin Sandys became more influential in the control of the colony.] Another interesting testimony to Puritanism in the Virginia Colony is the fact that Henry Jacob migrated there in 1622 and may have died there in 1624. [Daniel Neal, *History of the Puritans* (first published in 1731), is the only authority for the date and place of Jacob's death. The reference is from the 1837 edition of Thomas Tegg & Son, London, Vol. 1, p. 462.] Often the Puritan element in the early settlements in Virginia is obscured by the colony's later history and by the development of Massachusetts. Other examples of the shifts into which the Puritans were forced to evade the persecuting policy of Laud were (1) the attempt to buy up patronage and establish " lectures " in England (defeated by the work of Archbishop Laud and Bishop Wren), and (2) the development of the Puritan Classis in Holland, which was eventually suppressed by the intervention of the British Ambassador in the Netherlands, William Boswell. (Cf. Raymond Phineas Stearns, *Congregationalism in the Dutch Netherlands,* The American Society of Church History, Chicago, 1940, especially pp. 41–76.) Therefore, by the time the Civil War broke out in 1642, every move of the Puritans to circumvent Laud had been frustrated by the watchful eye of the Archbishop and the agents of the Crown. New England was their sole success, and few doubted that when Charles I and his bishops were a little less preoccupied it would receive full attention.

bar of Scripture, but also to construct on the basis of the New Testament the primitive and (to them) ideal pattern of the Church.[2]

These books did not go unread in England. They were circulated and discussed by many younger ministers who were already questioning the nature of the Church and were the more disposed to accept the views of men " martyred " for the Puritan cause[3] who, as they became convinced, found themselves faced with the same banishment and exile. The writings of Henry Jacob, Paul Baynes, Robert Parker and William Ames lead inevitably to the circuitous careers of such ministers as Hugh Peter, Thomas Hooker, John Davenport, John Cotton and the Apologists.

As one reads their story from this distance in history their cause appears to have been hopeless from the start, and yet the reader is forced to respect, even if he will not applaud, the tenacity with which they maintained their doctrine of the Church against all opposition, and the optimism with which they made new plans as soon as the vigilance of Laud and the efficiency of the King's agents blocked each one of their designs.[4]

At first they seem to have thought quite genuinely that they could reconcile this view of the Church with their formal acceptance

---

[2] E.g., Henry Jacob's *The Divine Beginning and Institution of Christ's True Visible or Ministerial Church* (1610), Paul Baynes's *The Diocesans Tryall* (1621), William Ames's *Medvlla Theologica* (1623). Ames's *Marrow of Sacred Divinity* did not appear in English until 1643. I have deliberately omitted titles dealing with Separatism or with ceremonial reform in the Church. They may easily be added from H. M. Dexter's invaluable bibliography, *The Congregationalism of the last three Hundred Years* (Harper, New York, 1880), Appendix.

[3] There is an amusing illustration of the prestige of Paul Baynes among Puritan students in Cambridge University in the Diary of Samuel Ward (who was later Lady Margaret Professor of Divinity and the third Master of Sidney Sussex College). Ward makes on Sept. 10, 1596, personal confession of " My pride in talking with Paul Baynes " (*Two Puritan Diaries,* edited by M. M. Knappen [American Soc. of Church Hist., 1933], p. 115). Paul Baynes had entered the lectureship at Great St. Andrews, which has previously been held by the famous Puritan, William Perkins, and Ward was at that time a student at Christ's College. In the same diary there is evidence of the Puritan reactions to the enforcement of the use of the surplice in college chapel. Cf. Ward's comments under the year 1604 in G. M. Edwards, *Sidney Sussex College* (1899), p. 68f.

[4] See the note on pp. 57–58 *supra.*

of the Royal Supremacy in matters of religion, and at the same time win for their doctrines acceptance within the general pattern of Reformed Churchmanship in Europe. However, the events that led up to the suppression of the English Classis in the Netherlands[5] should have convinced them, in Hugh Peter's words, that it " were as good to yeeld to the English Bishops as to the Dutch Classis."[6] The issue with Presbyterianism would appear to have been fairly joined. Yet when they returned to England at the outbreak of the struggle between Charles I and his Parliament, they seem to have thought that there was a reasonable chance either of persuading Parliament to adopt their views or at least of winning for themselves comprehension within a Reformed Church of England.

It must be remembered that the ecclesiastical situation in England at the outbreak of war in 1642 was extremely fluid. *The Root and Branch Petition* had been passed at the end of 1640, whereby the Parliament had asked that the episcopal government " with all its dependencies, roots and branches, may be abolished . . . and the government according to God's Word may be rightly placed amongst us,"[7] but there were many in Parliament who had been active in that parliamentary move who, like Oliver Cromwell, still had no clear idea what they wished to see in place of the old system.[8] Although those members of Parliament who remained in London were to a man Puritan in their religious sympathies and might be presumed to lean towards Presbyterianism, no one knew what their Puritanism would mean for the future shape of the Church in England, and this uncertainty undoubtedly gave the returned exiles some cause for hope, particularly since several

---

[5] R. P. Stearns, *Congregationalism in the Dutch Netherlands,* pp. 41–76.

[6] Goffe to Boswell, 7/17 April, 1634, from the *Boswell Papers,* re-printed in Proceedings of the *Massachusetts Historical Society,* XLII, p. 231.

[7] *Constitutional Documents of the Puritan Revolution 1625–1660* (Clarendon Press, Oxford, 1906, edited by S. R. Gardiner), p. 138.

[8] Cromwell had remarked to Sir Philip Warwick and Sir Thomas Chichely just about this time, " I can tell you, Sirs, what I would not have; tho' I cannot, what I would," Sir Philip Warwick's *Memoires of the Reigne of King Charles I* (1701), p. 176f. For a fuller survey of Cromwell's ecclesiastical uncertainty at this time see my account in *The Lord Protector* (Lutterworth Press, London, 1955), pp. 48–55.

influential leaders in Parliament were known to favor them.[9]

On the other hand, the constituency of the Westminster Assembly was heavily weighted on the Presbyterian side, and the dependence of the English Parliament on the military help of the Scots could only strengthen the hands of those who wanted England to copy the pattern of religious uniformity that had been established north of the border. Moreover, the Scots made their conditions for the alliance perfectly explicit.[10] The *Solemn League and Covenant* revealed the strength of the new wind in ecclesiastical matters, and the northern direction from which it was going to blow!

If the exiles had returned with any sanguine hopes for the speedy victory of their cause, the attitude of the Presbyterian majority in the Assembly and the active participation of the Scottish Commissioners must soon have convinced them otherwise. Furthermore, the express determination in the *Solemn League and Covenant* to extirpate "heresy, schism . . . and whatsoever shall be found to be contrary to sound doctrine and the power of godliness," while having their enthusiastic support in theory, took a somewhat different coloring when they discovered that they were among the heretics and schismatics to be purged. Their immediate task was quite clear: to establish the position they would take in the English Reformation they had to define their position between the Presbyterians on the one hand and the Separatists on the other; and one very effective non-theological factor which helped to determine the eventual character of Congregationalism in England was the Congregationalists' dilemma of preferring to be ecclesiastically in alliance with the Presbyterians, while politically they were forced to ally themselves with the Sects.

However, although many of the factors that eventually helped to shape Congregational views of the Church were admittedly due to the political circumstances in which the exiles and their followers found themselves in the England or New England of the mid-seventeenth century, the differences that emerged must not obscure the extent of their basic unity. The followers of "the Congrega-

---

[9] E.g., in the House of Lords, Lord Wharton and Lord Saye and Sele, and in the House of Commons, "young" Henry Vane, and the Solicitor, Oliver St. John.

[10] Gardiner, *Constitutional Documents,* p. 268. Cf. *infra* pp. 71ff.

tional Way " held in common a doctrine of the Church which they believed was fundamentally based upon Scripture,[11] and it was for this reason that this little band sweated and schemed in the Assembly, or schemed and sweated on the American frontier, to see that it was preserved.

We can no longer avoid the questions, what right have we to use the term " Congregational " in the seventeenth century? Who were the Congregationalists?

The answer to these questions must be prefaced with the reminder that we must distinguish between " Congregationalism " as a movement that has appeared within the Church *in* England, and the application of the term " Congregational " (to themselves) by a specific group of English Puritans within the Church *of* England. Or, to put the same issue in a slightly different form, we must distinguish between Congregationalism in its historical, geographical and spiritual inclusiveness today, and the men who may be precisely denominated " Congregational " in the first five decades of the seventeenth century.[12] The first of these alternatives in either case is much more inclusive than the second, having its own recognizable and formative pre-history, and taking within its orbit influences that need to be excluded when we consider those who

---

[11] I am in fundamental agreement with Dr. G. F. Nuttall when he points out that the basic appeal of seventeenth-century Congregationalism was neither to Calvin on the one hand nor Robinson on the other, but to the New Testament. The Dissenting Brethren could hardly have maintained themselves in the Assembly as long as they did if this had not been the case. (*Visible Saints,* Blackwell, Oxford, pp. 106, 143.) On the other hand this group sometimes quoted from their own " authorities." Thomas Hooker used the works of Ames and Parker to answer Paget, and although he undoubtedly thought these writers were at these fundamental points fully Scriptural, yet it was not quite the same as referring his opponent to the Scriptural source! Cf. Stearns, *Congregationalism in the Dutch Netherlands,* App. VIII, especially the answers to questions 14, 17.

[12] Champlin Burrage was careful to make this distinction. Writing of Robert Browne, he said, " Robert Browne, at an early stage of his career, may be truly called a pioneer of what *today* is known as Congregationalism, but a long period of evolution intervenes between him and present-day Congregationalists and Independents. His connection with the *first* Independents (or *first* Congregationalists) is likewise rather indirect." *The Early English Dissenters* (Cambridge University Press, Cambridge, 1912), I : 28.

first applied the term to themselves. It is unfortunate that some writers in this century have obscured these distinctions, and move from one use of the term to the other with a gay abandon which at times suggests that they acknowledge as valid history only those principles and personalities that they find congenial.[13]

Up to the appearance of Champlin Burrage's researches[14] the Congregational interpretation of its own history was universally agreed. Although there might be grounds for restrained scholarly argument as to whether Richard Fitz or Robert Browne deserved recognition as the " Father of Congregationalism," the main source of the origins was clear: it was " Brownism," which had its genesis in Elizabethan Separatism, and which came to be known to Shakespeare and the generality of Englishmen by the name of its most able exponent.[15] Any later groups which shared its view that in Christ's Church there was no superior spiritual authority on earth to the local covenanted fellowship of believers were seen simply as variations or developments of this movement.

Champlin Burrage placed a radical question mark against this traditional view. Among the sixty-four points for which he claimed fundamental revision in our estimate of early English dissent, he asserted that " The beginnings of Independency or Congregationalism, are not, as heretofore, traced to the Brownists or Barrowists, but to the Congregational Puritanism advocated by Henry Jacob and William Bradshaw about 1604 and 1605 . . . Puritan Congregationalism accordingly did not have its source in separatism, nor was it separatist in spirit, but was constantly declared by its upholders as involving a separation from the world, and not from the Church of England."[16] [Claim No. 61.]

The point must be conceded. We may criticize some of the details of Burrage's research,[17] or some of his more sweeping con-

---

[13] Of the dangers in this, see my article, " Shall we re-write our history?," *Congregational Quarterly*, Vol. XXXII, No. 3, July, 1954, pp. 234–40.

[14] Particularly in *The Early English Dissenters*.

[15] " Sir Andrew Aguecheek " in *Twelfth Night* (Act III, scene ii), " I had as lief be a Brownist as a politician."

[16] *The Early English Dissenters*, I : 33.

[17] E.g. Dr. Albert Peel examined critically Champlin Burrage's denial that Richard Fitz's London congregation could be regarded as the " first regularly constituted English Congregational Church " of which we have any record

tentions, but there seems to be little doubt that he was right in his main thesis that Congregationalism in the early seventeenth century refers specifically to a non-separatist movement[18] within the Puritan

---

[as Dr. R. E. Dale had suggested in *The History of English Congregationalism* (Hodder & Stoughton, London, 1907), pp. 92–95]. Cf. Peel, *The First Congregational Churches: New Light on Separatist Congregations in London 1567–81* (Cambridge University Press, Cambridge, 1920).

[18] See my article, "The Word 'Congregational': an historical footnote," in *The Hartford Quarterly*, Vol. IV, No. 1, Fall 1963, pp. 59ff. I suggest that John Cotton was the first to clarify the use of the word and claim it specifically as descriptive of the view of the Church that he represented (Cf. *The Way of the Congregational Churches Cleared*, p. 11.) Champlin Burrage had maintained that contrary to popular belief, instead of being persuaded by John Robinson to be a Separatist, Henry Jacob was never a Separatist, and was in fact the main instrument whereby Robinson "was won back from the ways of separatism before 1616 (certainly before 1618)," *The Early English Dissenters*, I:34, cf. *Ibid.*, pp. 290–95. Dr. Douglas Horton noted that the Leyden-Plymouth church "had become more tolerant with the passing years," to the extent that by 1617 the group was willing to recognize the validity of the Church of England's work and doctrine among its own parish members. (See the Introduction to the 1960 edition of *The Creeds and Platforms of Congregationalism*, pp. x–xi.) Champlin Burrage's position, however, has been accepted and developed by Verne D. Morey in his article "History corrects itself" (*Bulletin of the American Congregational Association* [The Congregational Library, Boston], Vol. 5, No. 2, January 1954, pp. 9–19). Although Dr. Burrage and Mr. Morey have good grounds for suggesting that Jacob influenced Robinson to modify his Separatism, rather than the other way about, it is to be questioned whether the reversion was as complete as they suggest. Verne Morey says that through his contact with Jacob, Robinson "finally went full circle by concluding that members of his church could, without censure, participate in public worship in the church of England. In later years his church was so far removed from normative Brownism that it often took communion with the Presbyterian church in Leyden." (*Op. cit.*, p. 16.) But John Cotton, who clearly admired John Robinson and would have liked to have been able to claim him as a convert to "Congregationalism," never went further than to say that it was "more than half way" (*The Way of the Congregational Churches Cleared* [London, 1648], p. 9). Furthermore, he explicitly asserts (against Robert Baillie's claim that Robinson had been their teacher) that they had their doctrine direct from the New Testament. (*Ibid.*) It is a pity that in quoting John Cotton's account of Robinson's spiritual pilgrimage — words which Cotton took from Baillie — Mr. Morey omits the crucial words that I have italicized, "hee came backe indeed the one halfe of the way: Acknowledging the lawfulnesse of communicating with the Church of England, *in Word*

wing of the Church of England. However much we may believe that Robert Browne and Elizabethan Separatism quite properly belong to the authentic pre-history of modern Congregationalism, it is to the pre-history that they belong, and they must be clearly distinguished from the Puritans who used the word " Congregational " to describe their own view of the Church.

This is where the *Apologeticall Narration* becomes important, for although the word " Congregational " does not appear in its pages, the Apologists later used it to describe the system of church government in which they believed[19] and it was constantly used by the authors who held to that system. The word " Congregational " is not used in the *Apologeticall Narration* itself, probably because the Dissenting Brethren were reluctant to define what they thought was the New Testament view of the Church in terms of any " ism," but they are careful to distinguish their doctrine of the Church from both Presbyterianism and Brownism. Clearly the following passage is of very great importance in this respect :[20]

> *That* proud and insolent title of *Independencie* was affixed unto us, as our claime; the very sound of which conveys to all mens apprehensions the challenge of an exemption of all Churches from all subjection and dependance, or rather a trumpet of defiance against what ever *Power, Spirituall* or *Civill;* which we doe abhor and detest: Or else the odious name of *Brownisme,* together with all their opinions as they have stated and maintained them, must needs be owned by us: Although upon the very first declaring our judgements in the chief and fundamental point of all *Church discipline,* and likewise since, it hath been acknowledged that we differ much from them. And wee did then, and

---

and *Prayer: but not in Sacraments and Discipline."* (*Ibid.,* p. 8.) Robinson may have moved a considerable distance from rigid Separatism (as Dr. Horton suggests), but his acceptance of the Church of England still had definite limits.

[19] E.g., Jeremiah Burroughs used the term the " Congregationall way " in 1646, *Irenicum,* p. 41, and Thomas Goodwin wrote later, "As the institution of a congregational church in Mat. xviii. most suits with Christ's aim and design, the communion of saints, so it most agrees too with that promise of his presence, ver. 20." (*On the Constitution . . . of the Churches of Christ, Works,* XI: 76.) Cf. " the congregational elders, the presbytery," " congregational assembly," " the congregational government," " a congregational church," *Ibid.,* pp. 75–80 *passim.*

[20] *Supra* p. 23f.

doe here publiquely professe, we beleeve the truth to lye and consist in a *middle way* betwixt that which is falsly charged on us, *Brownisme;* and that which is the contention of these times, the *authoritative Presbyteriall Government* in all the subordinations and proceedings of it.

However much they considered themselves to be simply within the general Reformed tradition, and however hesitant they were to distinguish their doctrine by a particular name, here was obviously a distinguishable view of the Church for which others would not be slow to provide the names if they did not find one for themselves. Therefore, part of the significance of the pamphlet is that it reveals the general agreement of its authors with the Congregational churchmanship which Cotton, Hooker and their colleagues were developing experimentally in America.

At the same time, the circumstances which caused the Apologists to petition the Houses of Parliament for freedom to enjoy the ordinances of Christ " with the allowance of a latitude to some lesser differences "[21] were pushing them to the point where in a mere fifteen years they would be prepared to recognize on a far wider basis " other churches (though less pure) to be true churches."[22] The exigencies of war that were to bring them willynilly into close contact and alliance with Brownists, Baptists and Separatists of all kinds, would also force these Puritan Englishmen to recognize the fuller ecumenical implications of that Christ-centered authority, which was at the heart of " the Congregational Way."

---

[21] *Supra* p. 31.

[22] *The Savoy Declaration* (1658), Platform of Polity, Art. XXX.

III

Religion, Politics and War

W E CANNOT separate the political and the religious aspects of
the civil wars in seventeenth-century England, and therefore the *Apologeticall Narration* must be seen not only as an important event in the emergence of a distinctive doctrine of the Church
but also as a significant incident in the struggle for power that was
developing within the parliamentary party during the year 1643–44.
It is because of the political and military overtones in the situation
itself that the words " Independent " and " Presbyterian " became
distinctive not merely of differing forms of church polity but of
two distinct political programs. A supporter of either of these
parties might have a leaning towards the ecclesiastical policy it
represented, but we must not think that all who became associated
with the " Independents " or the " Presbyterians " were inevitably
fervent adherents of any particular church system except in so far
as it contributed to the political or military program they happened
to favor.

It becomes particularly difficult to give a precise ecclesiastical
meaning to the term " Independent " because very early in the civil
war Independency as a political term began to cover the whole
spectrum of religious views. It ranged from comparatively orthodox Puritans like the Dissenting Brethren to followers of the most
bizarre of the rapidly burgeoning sects, or to *politiques* who had
little interest in church polity but feared the Scots and disliked the
prospect of uniformity. Professor A. S. P. Woodhouse observed that
it would be tempting to try and distinguish between the Presbyterians and the Independents of seventeenth-century England in terms
of Ernst Troeltsch's distinction between those who followed the
Puritan church-ideal (i.e., supporters of a State Church organization) and those who followed the Puritan sect-ideal (i.e., supporters
of the " gathered church " concept), but the problem of differentia-
tion breaks down among the Independents, who as a political party

"occupy . . . the whole interval between the Right, where the Puritan church-type is dominant, and the Left, where the Puritan sect-type is no less supreme." "No fact," comments Professor Woodhouse, "is more prominent than the existence of the two types side by side, or than their mutual influence particularly in the Centre Party, where indeed they merge."[1]

This mutual influence and merging was to be a major factor in modifying English Congregationalism during the seventeenth century. It prepared the way for the Restoration when all kinds of Independents, whether Puritan or Separatist, would be forced to accept the separation of Nonconformity, and when by proscription and persecution even Puritan Congregationalists would be forced into a form of Independent polity that was not altogether of their own choosing.

At the Restoration the issues were made very clear. It was no longer possible for Puritans of any color to maintain their loyalty to the national church with the continued practice of their own distinctive polities. They had the clear alternative, either to renounce their view of the Church and enter the Anglican episcopal system or to become Nonconformists. Even to convinced Congregationalists like Thomas Goodwin and John Owen the Separatist position became the more understandable and acceptable as they faced this issue themselves. Similarly, the sporadic persecution and constant proscription under which Nonconformity suffered made it virtually impossible for their system to exist in anything but the localized

---

[1] *Puritanism and Liberty* (J. M. Dent & Sons, London, 1938), Introduction, p. 36. Cf. Ernst Troeltsch, *The Social Teaching of the Christian Churches* (translated by Olive Wyon [Allen & Unwin, London and Macmillan, New York]), pp. 461ff. Troeltsch's distinction between the "church-type" and the "sect-type" has been an extremely valuable contribution in our understanding of the Church, but I would question whether his choice of terms was completely happy. They are certainly good enough if the Church is viewed in wholly sociological terms, but the word "sect" carries theological overtones that are pejorative and can be for that reason misleading. It implies a theological value-judgment, and it would have been preferable if he had used two terms that were more equivalent in their meaning. I suggest that "church-type" and "ecclesia-type" meets the case more exactly, since when the latter term is understood in its New Testament sense of a group "called out" it emphasizes the "gathered" nature of the Church. It also emphasizes the attempt of such religious groups to return to the New Testament ideal.

form of individual congregations. The meeting of synods or associations became entirely out of the question.[2]

In the alliances which brought the Independent party into being during the civil wars Congregationalists found themselves working for the same objectives as Separatists, Baptists, Fifth Monarchists and a host of smaller sects, and if at the Restoration this meant that they were the more ready to accept the logic of their own separation from Anglican episcopacy, it had also brought them to the point where the principle of toleration for all Christians had become an article of faith for them. This was a considerable modification of their earlier position, but we must notice that the ideas arose in the first instance not from their theological insights but from a political and military situation which made it imperative for all the smaller religious groups to unite in order to achieve and maintain the religious liberty that was their common objective.

Many of the differences that separated the Presbyterian and Independent parties find their source in the circumstances that surrounded the *Solemn League and Covenant* between England and Scotland. The summer of 1643 had been a grim time for the English Parliament — the Fairfaxes had been roundly defeated at Adwalton Moor (June 30th), Bristol and Exeter had been lost (July 26th, September 4th), Gloucester was undergoing a lengthy siege and was saved only at the last moment by the Earl of Essex (September 8th), while royalist plots and widespread agitation for an immediate peace settlement had grown in frequency and intensity among the citizenry of London itself. After the defeat of the Fairfaxes Parliament decided to dispatch four Commissioners headed by Sir Henry Vane the younger to try to persuade the Scots to enter the struggle on the side of the English Parliament. The Commissioners were accompanied by two ministerial representatives from the newly appointed Westminster Assembly of Divines,

---

[2] The issue became even more pointed, of course, with respect to the Presbyterians. As Daniel Neal remarked, " Little did the Presbyterian divines imagine, that in less than twenty years all their artillery would be turned against themselves; that they should be excluded from the establishment by an act of prelatical uniformity; that they should be reduced to the necessity of pleading for that indulgence which now they denied their brethren; and esteem it their duty to gather churches for separate worship out of others, which they allowed to be true ones." *History of the Puritans*, II : 381.

Stephen Marshall, and his son-in-law, Philip Nye, who was to be one of the Apologists.

The Commissioners went to Scotland to negotiate an alliance between the two kingdoms, but at once a very real difference of approach revealed itself in the discussions. It must be remembered that although religion had an important place in the struggle between Charles and his English Parliament, the most important issues at the beginning of the conflict were constitutional. In Scotland the opposite had been true, for the issue there had come to its head in Charles's attempts to establish episcopacy and the Book of Common Prayer on the Scottish Kirk. Robert Baillie made the significant comment at the beginning of the negotiations between the two countries that the English " were for a civill League, we for a religious Covenant."[3] All the later friction between the two nations during the Civil War was in this difference of approach to the *Solemn League and Covenant,* for the English regarded themselves as negotiating an alliance between two sovereign states in which religion ought properly to be the domestic concern of each, whereas the Scots thought more in terms of a covenant between two national Kirks.

It has been pointed out that the English Parliament would never relinquish " that control of the clergy by the laity which had been the most abiding result of Tudor rule,"[4] but at that moment all the cards were stacked in the Scots' favor, and Baillie and his friends very soon showed that they would do nothing for the English parliamentary cause unless the English Commissioners were prepared at least to acquiesce in the aims of the Church of Scotland. The Commissioners had no choice but to accept the terms which the Scots proposed.

It is clear that the Scots were aware that there were those in England who deviated from the Presbyterian form of Puritan ecclesiology. They dubbed them " Independents " — the term they used for Separatists. When the news arrived in Scotland (in July 1643) that the English were thinking of opening negotiations for an alliance, Robert Baillie had observed that " Mr. Marshall will

---

[3] To William Spang, September 22, 1643, *Letters and Journals,* II : 90.
[4] S. R. Gardiner, *The Great Civil War* (1893 edition; Longman's, Green & Co., London, 4 vols.), I : 228.

be most welcome, bot if Mr. Nye, the head of the independants, be his fellow, we cannot take it weell."[5] Robert Baillie, who for some time had been engaged in writing an attack on Brownism,[6] went on to say that Robert Meldrum had been deputed to find out for the Scots " what wee may expect from them anent uniformitie of Church Government; if in this he bring no satissfaction to us quicklie, it will be a great impediment to their affaires here."[7]

There was a good deal of hard bargaining before the *Solemn League and Covenant* was signed. Baillie testified " we had hard enough debates."[8] A considerable number of the Scots were for remaining uncommitted, with the possibility of offering their services as arbiters between both sides in England, until Archibald Johnston of Warriston convinced them of the futility of that policy. However, they remained suspicious of the English Parliament's attitude on matters of religion, and it was particularly noted by Baillie that the Commissioners in Scotland were, " more nor we could assent to, for keeping of a doore open in England to Independencie."[9] This is hardly surprising in view of Vane and Nye's presence among the Commissioners, or indeed in view of the leadership that the Independents were giving to the Parliamentary cause. Henry Vane, however, does not appear to have been suspected by the Scots at this point,[10] but the fact that he had taken a leading part in negotiating the *Solemn League and Covenant* explains why the Scots regarded his eventual stand for religious toleration in the nature of treachery.[11]

A price was being set for Scottish military help, and it was a figure far in excess of the £30,000 per month and £100,000 (in advance) which the Scots demanded for their participation. Eng-

---

[5] Letter to William Spang, July 26, 1643, *Letters and Journals,* II: 81.

[6] Letter to Spang, July 26, 1643, *Ibid.,* p. 76.

[7] *Ibid.,* p. 81.

[8] To the same, September 22, *Ibid.,* p. 90.

[9] *Ibid.*

[10] Even in April 1644 Baillie wrote, " Sir Harie Vane, whatever his judgment, yet less nor more, does not owne them (the Independents of the Assembly), and gives them no encouragement." Public Letter, April 2nd, 1644, *Ibid.,* p. 146.

[11] Cf. *Ibid.,* pp. 230, 235.

land had to settle for the establishment of Scottish Presbyterian uniformity in England and Ireland, and lest there should be any doubt about the intention it was expressly laid down in the first article of the *Solemn League and Covenant*:

> That we shall sincerely, really and constantly, through the grace of God, endeavour in our several places and callings, the preservation of the reformed religion in the Church of Scotland, in doctrine, worship, discipline and government, against our common enemies; the reformation of religion in the kingdoms of England and Ireland, in doctrine, worship, discipline and government, according to the Word of God, and the example of the best reformed Churches; and we shall endeavour to bring the Churches of God in the three kingdoms to the nearest conjunction and uniformity in religion, confession of faith, form of Church government, directory for worship and catechising, that we, and our posterity after us, may, as brethren, live in faith and love, and the Lord may delight to dwell in the midst of us.

The wording of this document[12] indicates what the Scots regarded as the normative pattern of the " reformed religion " that was to be professed in the three kingdoms, for by it the English Parliament was engaged to endeavor the " preservation " of the form established in Scotland, and the " reformation " of the Church in England and Ireland in conformity with that ideal. Owing to the urgency of the military situation the English Commissioners were in no position to hold out indefinitely, and the best Vane could do was to secure the provision that the projected reformation should be " according to the Word of God."[13] Even the Scottish ministers could hardly find any valid reason for refusing to accept this. It was a slim enough life-line for the Independents, but it must be remembered that the Independents claimed that their whole ecclesiology had been based simply on the Scriptural pattern of the Church. They made good use of this in the debates within the Westminster Assembly.

In fact, the phrasing of the *Solemn League and Covenant* throws a great deal of light on the form in which the Independents made their protest in the Assembly. It explains the anxiety of

---

[12] S. R. Gardiner (ed.), *Constitutional Documents of the Puritan Revolution 1625–1660* (Oxford, 1906 edition), p. 268.

[13] The reasons for attributing this to Vane is given by S. R. Gardiner in *The Great Civil War*, I: 230 f., note.

Baillie and his colleagues to gain support from Protestants abroad, and the insistence of the Dissenting Brethren and their sympathizers in New England that what they desired in the Church was in conformity with the " example of the best reformed churches." But the primary question was which form of church government was most nearly " according to the Word of God." This was the fundamental issue, and the *Apologeticall Narration,* no less than the Dissenting Brethren's vocal agitation within the Assembly, was a public claim to recognition and toleration on the ground that the Congregational form of the Church was more true to the Word of God than the Presbyterian system in Scotland. Vane's amendment, seemingly so innocuous, was to be the basis of their opposition to Presbyterian uniformity. It opened a small enough " door " for the Independents in England, but it was sufficient — at least until the military situation gave more cogent practical reasons to guarantee toleration.

The national situation which produced the *Solemn League and Covenant,* Westminster Assembly and the protest voiced in the *Apologeticall Narration* very rapidly revealed other deep cleavages that were distinct from the ecclesiastical differences at issue, but which seem to have found their focus in them.

In the first place there was the reaction in favor of English nationalism. The military and political situation had produced the *Solemn League and Covenant.* But this resulted in an inevitable reaction, and English national feeling became a factor which seriously threatened the unity of the parliamentary opposition to the King. The rivalry became increasingly apparent during the course of the war, and it was often turned to good account by Charles who skillfully played off the interests of the two countries against each other. England and Scotland were separate nations that had been constitutionally united for less than fifty years and their union was only in a common allegiance to the royal (but Scottish) house of Stuart. They had far too recent and far too extensive a history as hereditary enemies to be amenable to any attempt by one nation to exert undue influence upon the internal affairs of the other. In 1642–43 the English desperately needed the help of the Scots and there was enough in their common plight to keep them together, but in so far as Presbyterian uniformity seemed to be the

73

imposition of a foreign system upon England it was bound to be resented. In providing the nucleus of opposition to the Scots, the Independents to a degree became the party that represented English national independence.

A further rift that rapidly threatened the unity of Parliament was that which developed between the House of Lords and the House of Commons. The leadership in the first political moves against the Crown had come from the Commons — Pym, Hampden, Holles, Stroud were all members of the Commons — but with the outbreak of hostilities the peers asserted their traditional role on the field of battle. The Earl of Essex became Commander-in-Chief, and several of the other peers who were loyal to Parliament assumed leadership in the field almost as by hereditary right. It soon became clear, however, that the two houses of Parliament represented somewhat different objectives in waging war against the King. The Lords fought rather in the spirit of the barons against King John, not to defeat the King and change the traditional constitution of the country, but to maintain their own privileges by curbing the power of the Crown and by appointing royal advisers of their own choosing. Ostensibly this was also the intention of the Commons, but the Commons rapidly began to assume duties and an authority far in excess of that which it enjoyed under the old constitution. New and revolutionary ideas of parliamentary sovereignty began to be heard, and the House of Commons began to assert a new status for its members as the elected representatives of the People. Among the politically minded troopers of the army advanced concepts of the sovereignty of the People gained ground and were in constant debate. The majority of members in the House of Commons undoubtedly leaned towards Presbyterianism, but they were not averse to augmenting the prestige of the Commons at the expense of the Lords, and in so far as the Independent party had its best leadership in the Commons it found itself more and more ranged against the interests of the peers and turned to the House of Commons for its support. It rarely turned to that House in vain. Moreover, because of its influence in the Commons, it was able to represent the aspirations of the more radical and popular elements that were vocal in the ranks of the army.

These differences come to a focus in another bitter struggle which developed in military circles very rapidly and finally broke in the late autumn of 1644. It represented a radical difference of opinion in the way that the war should be conducted. The Presbyterian party, represented by the Earl of Essex, the Scots, and the General of the Army of the Eastern Association, the Earl of Manchester, stood for an essentially conservative policy politically and an essentially defensive policy militarily. Against this Oliver Cromwell, supported by the Independents in the Army and in Parliament, stood for the policy of seeking out and destroying the King's army and hence his ability to wage war.

Throughout the last few months of 1643 and the beginning of 1644 this explosive difference continued to grow, and first sputtered into flame in Cromwell's dispute with Laurence Crawford, the Scottish Major-General of the Earl of Manchester's army. Cromwell himself had been appointed Lieutenant-General (i.e., Commander of cavalry) of the Army of the Eastern Association on January 21st, 1644, and he had also become a member of the Committee of Both Kingdoms, in which the supreme direction of the war was vested, when the Committee was formed in February of that year. With the creation of this committee Scotland became officially involved in the English war, and Crawford had been appointed to the Eastern Association. He seems rapidly to have supplanted Cromwell in the confidence of the Earl of Manchester and stiffened Manchester's Presbyterian prejudices. It is significant that the first sign of Cromwell's dispute with Crawford is to be found in a letter in which he protested against the latter's treatment of an officer who had been dismissed for being an Anabaptist.[14] This minor spat flared to a head in September of the same

---

[14] " Surely you are not well advised to turn off one so faithful to the Cause, and so able to serve you as this man is. Give me leave to tell you, I cannot be of your judgment. . . .

Aye, but the man is an Anabaptist. Are you sure of that? Admit he be, shall that render him incapable to serve the public. He is indiscreet. It may be so, in some things, we have all human infirmities. I tell you, if you had none but such indiscreet men about you, and would be pleased to use them kindly, you would find them as good a fence to you as any you have yet chosen.

Sir, the State, in choosing men to serve them, takes no notice of their opinions, if they be willing faithfully to serve them, that satisfies. I advised you formerly to bear with men of different minds from yourself. . . . Take heed of being

year, but died down rapidly when the House of Commons — to Robert Baillie's extreme disgust — passed an order virtually guaranteeing the principle of religious toleration.[15] It was, however, but an opening salvo in the more important quarrel that issued in Cromwell's impeachment of the Earl of Manchester and produced the Self-Denying Ordinance and a complete change in the direction of the war.[16]

In the quarrel between Cromwell and the Earl of Manchester, which broke out in November 1644, the tensions that underlay all the other differences in the parliamentary party were brought to light.[17] Cromwell charged Manchester with having " alwayes been indisposed and backward to Engagements, and against the ending of the War by Sword," with acting " as if he thought the King too low, and Parliament too high,"[18] and with having declared publicly that " if we beate the King 99 times he would be King still, and his posterity, and we his subjects still; but if he beate us but once we should be hang'd and our posterity be undone."[19] One can see how convictions like these held by those in the chief places of command

---

sharp, or too easily sharpened by others, against those to whom you can object little but that they square not with you in every opinion concerning matters of religion." March 10th, 1643/4, *Writings and Speeches of Oliver Cromwell,* I : 278.

[15] " While Cromwell is here, the House of Commons, without the least advertisement to any of us, or of the Assemblie, passes an order, that the grand committee of both Houses, Assemblie, and us, shall consider of the means to unite us and the Independents ; or, if that be found impossible, to see how they might be tollerate. This hes much affected us." Letter to D. Dickson, 16th September, 1644, *Letters and Journals,* II : 230. (Cf. the letter to Spang, September 13th, *Ibid.* p. 226.)

[16] First proposed on December 9th, 1644, but it was not finally ratified by the House of Lords until February 15th, 1644/5.

[17] I have dealt with the events that led up to this quarrel in more detail in *The Lord Protector* (Lutterworth Press, London, 1955), pp. 71–93. The most detailed documentary treatment is to be found in *The Quarrel between the Earl of Manchester and Oliver Cromwell* (Camden Society, 1875), edited by John Bruce and David Masson.

[18] John Rushworth, *Historical Collections* (7 vols., 1659–1701), VI : 732.

[19] Cromwell's Narrative in *The Quarrel between the Earl of Manchester and Oliver Cromwell,* p. 65.

would frustrate all decisive military action. On the other hand Cromwell was charged by Manchester[20] with having said that

> he hoped to live to see never a Nobleman in England, and he loved such better than others because they did not love lords. He had further expressed himselfe wth contempt of the Assembly of Divines, to whome I pay a reverence, as to the most learned and godly convention that hath bin this many ages, yett these he termed persecutors; and that they persecuted honester men than themselves. His animositie against that Scottish nation . . . was such as he told me that in the way they now carried themselves, pressing for their discipline, he could as soone draw sword against them as against any in the King's army . . .

We can see here the relationship between political strategy, national prejudice and military policy in the mind of Cromwell, and how they came to a focus for him in the Scots' intention to enforce Presbyterian uniformity. At this stage of the war the Independent party was the nucleus around which were gathered those who resented the growing influence of Scotland over her southern neighbor, those political radicals who questioned the traditional three orders of the Constitution, those who detested the uniformity proposed by the Westminster Assembly, and above all, those who had nothing to lose and everything to gain by pursuing the war to decisive victory.

From the *Solemn League and Covenant* of September 1643 to the first proposal of the Self-Denying Ordinance in December 1644 is a bare fifteen months, but it was time enough to bring all the issues between the Presbyterian and Independent parties in England to a head. Charles I realized very soon that the differences presented him with a wonderful opportunity to exercise the diplomatic skills in which the Stuarts always regarded themselves as adept, and after his capture in April 1646, he spent the next eighteen months in playing off the two parties against each other. But he had recognized the potential value to his cause from the very first, and almost at the same time as the *Apologeticall Narration* was appearing in print, a special meeting of the Assembly was

---

[20] Manchester's accusation against Cromwell in the *Camden Miscellany*, VIII; cf. Mrs. S. C. Lomas's note in her edition of Carlyle's *Oliver Cromwell's Letters and Speeches* (3 vols., G. P. Putnam's Sons, New York, 1906), I: 184.

convened on Saturday, 27th January, 1643/4, at the request of the House of Lords, to hear a report from Lord Wharton, Philip Nye, and John Goodwin on an attempt by the King to win the support of the Independents. The overtures had been made through a royalist prisoner, Ogle, and it had been suggested that the Independents should unite with " the moderate Protestant " (i.e., Episcopalians) against Presbyterianism. Since the Independents held the allegiance of an increasingly important part of the parliamentary army, such an alliance might very well have been decisive.[21] Lord Wharton's report on these moves shows that at this stage the Independents were being very " correct " in emphasizing their adherence to the common cause, but after some experience of the shifts and maneuvers employed by the more intractable Presbyterians in Parliament to gain their point absolutely, they became a little less punctilious about treating with the King to secure their own terms.

During this period the Independent leaders learned some of their most important political lessons, and if the first was the recognition by the Congregationalists that in order to win their own toleration they must be willing to extend it to others, the second was that if they were to enjoy this liberty in England they would have to forge their own military weapon to defend it.[22] Therefore, it is the period of Cromwell's rapid rise to military recognition, of the successful minor engagements in 1643 at Grantham (May), Burleigh House (July), the relief of Gainsborough (July), and Winceby (October). It was followed by the great victory of Marston Moor in July 1644, in which the Independents were not slow to claim that Cromwell had been the " Saviour of the Three Kingdoms."[23] Furthermore, 1643 had seen the tragic deaths of several like Pym and Hampden, who had been great leaders in the parliamentary cause. The way was open for new leadership, and

---

[21] S. W. Carruthers, *The Everyday Work of the Westminster Assembly*, p. 7, Baillie to Spang, Feb. 18th, 1643/4, *Letters and Journals*, II : 137. It seems from this letter also that " the appearance of a breach with the Independents " was more generally recognized by the Presbyterians about this time. *Ibid.*, p. 130f.

[22] Cf. *The Lord Protector*, pp. 76–78.

[23] Cf. the extract from Nathaniel Fiennes's *Vindiciae Veritatis, Ibid.*, p. 401, or in the *English Historical Review*, No. 18 (April 1890), Vol. V, p. 351f.

clearly Oliver Cromwell was emerging as "the great Independent."[24]

This, then, and the sequel in the unsatisfactory battle of Newbury (October) which set off the charges against Manchester, is the background of military events against which the deliberations of the Westminster Assembly must be set. It was a struggle for power within the parliamentary party which was carried on upon all fronts short of open war itself, and in the midst of a civil war in which both Presbyterians and Independents were engaged to the death against the King. The publication of the *Apologeticall Narration* came comparatively early in the sequence of events, and for that reason it bears a significance out of all proportion to its size, for it identified an ecclesiastical alternative to that which was being proposed in the Assembly. The men who wrote it and their supporters in the Assembly and in Parliament represented the leadership around which an effective opposition to the Scots, the Peers, and the Presbyterians might gather.

What was done in the Assembly was clearly more in the realm of theology than that of politics, but we cannot ignore the *political* significance of the struggle that took place there. Moreover, there is very good evidence to show that the Dissenting Brethren were fully conscious of this aspect of their work and acted in the closest cooperation with the political and military leaders of the Independent party. Robert Baillie complained repeatedly about the deliberate way in which this small group of divines held up the debates in the Assembly and prevented effective action. Time was on their side, and they knew it. Their policy was to prevent any premature recommendation of Presbyterian uniformity to Parliament by the Assembly until Cromwell and his troops had had the chance to demonstrate their indispensability in the war against the King. The value of these troops to the parliamentary cause was fully shown in the battle of Marston Moor (July 2nd, 1644), and the Independents in Parliament and outside it made the most of their opportunity. It is significant that when Cromwell appeared at Westminster in September to press his charges against Major-General Crawford, the House of Commons meekly passed the required guarantee of toleration and the charges against Crawford were immediately

---

[24] Baillie, Public Letter, April 2nd, 1644, *Letters and Journals,* II : 153.

dropped. Robert Baillie thought that the charges against Crawford were dropped because of clever management on the part of the Scottish Commissioners; however, it was not the dismissal of Crawford which the Independents wanted but a clear statement from the House of Commons on the question of their toleration.[25] Through the astute management of that matter in the House by Sir Henry Vane and Oliver St. John, through the brilliant victory of Cromwell and his troops at Marston Moor, and through the academic obstruction patiently carried out by the Dissenting Brethren in the Westminster Assembly, they won their point.

---

[25] To William Spang, October 25th, 1644, *Letters and Journals,* II : 235.

IV

The Dissenting Brethren

THOMAS FULLER in his account of the parties in the Westminster Assembly reminds us that the " Dissenting Brethren " suffered several different names of opprobrium. Some spoke of them as Separatists, and others called them Independents, although they themselves, said Fuller, if they are summoned by that name, " will return no *Vous avez*[1] thereunto, as to a word odious and offensive in the common sound thereof."[2]

Fuller deprecated the use of " such words of distaste," and his catholic spirit no less than his historical sense urges the reader to caution even in accepting his testimony because he recognized that he had to rely a good deal on " what we have collected out of the writings of pens professedly engaged against them." Bearing in mind Fuller's own ecclesiastical preferences, we feel that he treats them very fairly. He perhaps offers us a brief glimpse of the way in which the bitterness of the civil war had been often softened by small acts of personal consideration, when he confessed his own " personal respects to some of the afore-named Dissenters for favours received from them."[3]

We know that the five divines[4] who signed the *Apologeticall Narration* were not the sole representatives of their particular ecclesiology in the Assembly, as Fuller seems to have implied; and yet the fact that the royalist historian wrote about them in this way is a witness to their obvious pre-eminence among their own party. " These ' Dissenting Brethren,' or ' Congregationalists,' " declared Fuller, " were but five in the Assembly, though many more of their

---

[1] I.e., Vous avez raison — You are right!

[2] *Church History,* III: 461 (Bk. XI. S V. 35–41.)

[3] All but the first three books of Fuller's *Church History* were written during the Commonwealth and Protectorate period, when men like Goodwin and Nye were in positions where they could often help needy royalists.

[4] They were sometimes linked with William Greenhill and William Carter as the " septemvirs " — the seven who signed *The Reasons of the Dissenting Brethren against the Third Proposition concerning Presbyterial Government* (1645).

judgments dispersed in the land; namely, 1. Thomas Goodwin, bred first in Christ's College, then Fellow of Catherine Hall in Cambridge; 2. Philip Nye, who had his education in Oxford; 3. William Bridge, Fellow of Emmanuel College in Cambridge, all three still alive; 4. Sidrach Simpson, of Queen's College in Cambridge; 5. Jeremiah Burroughs, of Emmanuel College in Cambridge, both deceased."[5] These were the men who remained in the memory as personifying the Independent position by their protest in 1643-44.

All these men had at one time or another been associated with the Puritan congregations at Arnheim or Rotterdam in the Netherlands. Thomas Edwards was not slow in alluding to this. " In *Holland*," he reminds them, " there were but two Churches of your way and communion, one of which was at *Rotterdam* where M[r] *Bridge* and M[r] *Sympson* were members, and afterward M[r] *Burroughs*. . . . The other Church was first at *Viana* [sic], then at *Arnhim* [sic], of which M[r] *Goodwin* and M[r] *Nye* were Teachers. . . ."[6] These congregations had a special importance in the history of non-separatist Congregationalism, particularly the Church at Rotterdam, which Hugh Peter[7] had re-organized as a gathered and covenanted church early in 1633 and where he had been joined by the redoubtable Dr. William Ames as Teacher in the summer of the same year.[8] These churches had an open and acknowledged relationship to each other;

---

[5] *Ibid.* Simpson had died in 1655, and Burroughes in 1646. Brief biographies of all five of the Apologists are given in the *Dictionary of National Biography* (London, Smith, Elder & Co., 1885 *et seq.*), edited by Leslie Stephan (and later by Sir Sidney Lee; referred to as *D.N.B.*). Brief biographies of Nye, Goodwin and Bridge are also given by A. G. Matthews in *Calamy Revised: Being a Revision of Edmund Calamy's Account of the Ministers and others ejected and silenced 1660–62* (Clarendon Press, Oxford, 1934). Although the accounts in *Calamy Revised* are briefer than the articles in the *D.N.B.*, A. G. Matthews has been able to correct our knowledge of these men in certain details and adds other important information.

[6] *Antapologia*, p. 35.

[7] Hugh Peter or Peters. His name appears in both forms.

[8] Ames did not remain long, for he died within the same year. But the fact that he was prepared to remove himself from his Chair in the University of Franeker to start a new college associated with Peter's church at Rotterdam is itself significant. Cf. Stearns, *Congregationalism in the Dutch Netherlands*, pp. 54–56, 71.

and their significance is within this relationship, for the leaders were trying to break through the rigid independency of limiting church discipline to individual congregations, to which the concept of the Covenanted Church had been hitherto restricted in Separatism.

Thomas Goodwin (1600–80)

The intellectual and academic prestige of Thomas Goodwin among the Independents is indicated by the royalist chronicler, Anthony Wood, who links the name of Goodwin with that of John Owen as " the two Atlasses and Patriarchs of Independency."[9] But the circumstances that led Thomas Goodwin — and his colleague in the Westminster Assembly, Philip Nye — to stray from the comparatively safe path of English Puritanism into the more exacting pilgrimage of the Congregational Way, is of more than usual interest for both sides of the Atlantic. It illustrates in a rather dramatic way the closely spun skein of personal influences that linked the leaders of the movement in England and America.

As indicated by Fuller, Thomas Goodwin had been educated at Cambridge,[10] and apparently became a great admirer of Dr. John Preston, whom he eventually succeeded as Lecturer at Trinity Church. Preston had been extremely popular with the Puritan students in Cambridge during the last decade of James I's reign, but Cotton Mather claims that even the renowned Dr. Preston had been " pierced to the heart " by a sermon preached in St. Mary's by a young scholar named John Cotton. Mather therefore claims that his maternal grandfather had become " a spiritual father unto one of the greatest men of his age," and although we may have to discount this estimate as family hero-worship, it does seem clear that Preston entered into regular consultation and friendship with Cotton from this period and directed some of his best students to him.[11]

---

[9] *Athenae Oxonienses* (London, 2nd edition, 1721), II: 738. Anthony Wood (sometimes written " Anthony à Wood ") made his account complete from 1500 to the year of his own death, 1695.

[10] A. B. 1616–17; A.M. 1620, Fellow of St. Catharine's; S.T.B. 1630; President of Magdalen College, Oxford, 1650; D.D. (Oxon.) 1653.

[11] *Magnalia Christi Americana; or the Ecclesiastical History of New-England* [first published in London, 1702]. Citation is from the Hartford edition (Silas Andrus & Son) of 1855, I: 256–61.

When at last pressure from the episcopal authorities had become so great that Cotton determined to leave England, he traveled to London with the intention of sailing to Holland. He was dissuaded from this project by the advice of Thomas Hooker — doubtless based upon the increasing difficulties besetting the classis of English Congregationalists, which were due to the diplomacy of the King's ambassador and the growing suspicion of the Dutch authorities.[12] Cotton therefore determined to emigrate to New England, but some of his Puritan friends in London arranged a conference in which they tried to persuade him to conform to the " indifferent " ceremonies of the English Church. Goodwin and Nye were two who were present, and what then happened is described by Cotton Mather :[13]

> *Then* he gave his arguments for his non-conformity, and the reasons why he must rather forgo his *ministry,* or at least his *country,* than wound his *conscience* with unlawful compliances ; the issue whereof was, that instead of bringing Mr. Cotton back to what he had now forsaken, he brought them off altogether from what they had hitherto practised : every one of those eminent persons — Dr. Goodwin, Mr. Nye, and Mr. Davenport — now became all that he was, and at last left the kingdom for their being so.

John Owen, who was later to become the acknowledged intellectual leader of English Congregationalism, also admitted that his own conversion to the Congregational Way had been due to reading one of Cotton's books.[14] If Thomas Goodwin and Philip Nye had similarly succumbed to the persuasive logic of John Cotton, we have an extremely important link in the chain of personal relationships that joined the Puritans of New England to those who shared their views in the homeland. We also have clear evidence of Cotton's importance in the development of the whole movement.

---

[12] Stearns, *Congregationalism in the Dutch Netherlands,* chapters IV and V.

[13] *Magnalia,* I : 264.

[14] See *supra* p. 55f., note 34. Owen was never a member of the Westminster Assembly, as I inadvertently made him in *The Atonement and the Sacraments* (p. 117). When writing of the Assembly in his *Answer to Stillingfleet,* Owen expressly declared, " I was none of them." (*Works,* XV : 433.) I am grateful to a former student, the Reverend Geoffrey Barnes of Australia, for pointing out my slip. Happy is the teacher who is kept humble by his students !

Thomas Goodwin had become Lecturer (or public Preacher) at Trinity Church in Cambridge upon the death of Dr. Preston in 1628, and in 1632 he accepted the official position of Vicar. It seems, however, from the account in the *Magnalia*, that it was only about a year after taking this position that he became convinced of the rightness of John Cotton's course.[15] He resigned his living in 1634, and for the next few shadowy years he seems to have lived in and about London. By 1639, however, the constant harrying of Archbishop Laud's agents had made him cross the sea to Holland and settle at Arnheim, where Philip Nye had already held the charge of a small congregation of Englishmen since 1633. Therefore, for a short time, until the opening of the Long Parliament (November 3rd, 1640) enabled them to return with some hope to England, Goodwin and Nye were close colleagues in the pastorate at Arnheim.

The beginning of the Parliament's open struggle with Charles I not only made their cause respectable but even honorable. Having returned to their homeland, both men were nominated to the Westminster Assembly, and from the first they were recognized as leaders of the Independent group — indeed, Anthony Wood suggests that the *Apologeticall Narration* was actually written by Goodwin and Nye alone.[16] As the political and military influence of their party progressed they were both marked out for positions of importance in Church and State. On arriving in England Goodwin had gathered a Congregational Church at St. Dunstan-in-the-East in London, but with the rapid rise of Cromwell after the execution of Charles I, he was appointed preacher to the Council of State in 1649, and in 1650 Parliament nominated him to be President of Magdalen College, Oxford. In 1653 he became a member of the commission that was appointed for the approbation of ministers (a " Trier "), and in the following year assisted those who were appointed to eject scandalous ministers and schoolmasters in the county of Oxfordshire (an " Ejector "). In December 1653 he was made a D.D. of Oxford University.

---

[15] Cotton crossed the Atlantic in 1633 (with Hooker and Stone), but in 1647 he invited Thomas Goodwin to New England. Goodwin was dissuaded by his friends (*D.N.B. ad loc.*), but the incident illustrates the close relationship between Cotton and Goodwin.

[16] *Athenae Oxon.*, II : 504.

Thomas Goodwin thus received many of the modest honors and a good deal of the effectual power that were open to Congregational clergymen in Republican England. But although he was influential at Westminster and even more influential later at the Protector's court at Whitehall, he seems to have devoted his best energies to theological writing and the training of students. No seventeenth-century head of a college entered into his duties with more seriousness or with deeper pastoral concern.

The center of this concern was in the regular Congregational "Church Meeting" which he instituted in the President's Lodgings at Magdalen College. Although it was not for some years that Goodwin's own definitive exposition of Congregational churchmanship was to be published,[17] the "Church" which he gathered in Magdalen is a witness both to the seriousness with which he held his ecclesiological views and to his pastoral concern for students. From Anthony Wood's remark that "all those that were to enter into that Fraternity were openly to make Confession of their sins,"[18] we can surmise that this was a regularly convenanted fellowship based upon Confession of Faith and under the discipline of a regular Church Meeting.

However, Goodwin appears to have maintained a surprisingly catholic breadth in the membership of the college "gathered church." Theophilus Gale (who became tutor to the sons of Lord Wharton after the Restoration) was a member, as was Zachary Mayne who often preached at its weekly meetings.[19] We learn that as a student of Presbyterian views, John Howe did not initially offer himself for membership but that Goodwin persuaded him to join without prejudicing in any sense Howe's ecclesiastical position.[20] Even more surprising in view of Goodwin's extensive defense of orthodox Calvinism was his treatment of Zachary Mayne in the face of the Socinian doubts which Mayne claims he had always held:

---

[17] *Of the Constitution, Right Order, and Government of the Churches of Christ.*

[18] Wood, *Fasti Oxoniensis,* II: 104.

[19] Wood, *Athenae Oxon.,* II: 607, 919.

[20] Alexander Gordon in *D.N.B.*

Dr. *Goodwin* was indeed a very great Friend, and as a Father to me. I lived in the same College with him seven Years, and was of the number of those that joined with him as an Independent Congregation, and accordingly was pitched by him to be a Lecturer in *Shrewsbury* in *Shropshire,* and to promote the Congregational way. . . . All the seven Years that I was in the College with Dr. *Goodwin,* I was (by the Grace of God) working myself out of Enthusiasm, which I had deeply imbib'd from my Infancy: and I frequently threw in Objections in our Meetings (which were once a Week under *Dr. Goodwin's* Superintendency) where we discoursed *Ex tempore* upon a Divinity Question. — At last I made a solemn Proposal to Dr. *Goodwin* to be dismiss'd from their Society, or rather declared to him that I judged not my self as obliged to them more than to others by any relation I had entred into as a Member of their Society: and I remember his answer was, *he would not dismiss me into the World,* &c.[21]

Zachary Mayne commented that although he had for some time been in the process of accepting the Socinian position, he had received plenty of assurances in 1658 that he could have obtained episcopal ordination " upon such Terms as I should be satisfied in."[22] Goodwin's leniency towards Mayne's doubts is certainly not to be explained in terms of latitudinarianism of that kind. No one was less likely to look with favor upon any doctrine that threw doubt upon the orthodox doctrine of the Trinity. Mayne himself seems to explain Goodwin's attitude to him in a very different way — as arising out of Goodwin's real pastoral care for an individual student.

Thomas Goodwin stood very high in Oliver Cromwell's esteem, and throughout the Protectorate period (1653–58) he was close to the center of government. Cromwell had been proclaimed and installed as Lord Protector on the 16th December, 1653, and on the 30th of the same month the new administration held a solemn ceremony of humiliation before God when Thomas Goodwin joined with Cromwell's chaplains at Whitehall, Peter Sterry and Nicholas Lockyer, in the sermons and prayers.[23] According to Wood, Goodwin exercised a very considerable influence on Cromwell in the

---

[21] Quoted by Wood, *Athenae Oxon.,* II : 919–20.

[22] *Ibid.,* p. 919.

[23] Abbott, *Writings and Speeches of Oliver Cromwell,* III : 157.

measures taken to regulate the universities,[24] and he was one of the small group of clergymen, which also included Nye and Owen,[25] who were called in to advise the Protector on Manasseh ben Israel's proposal that the Jews should be allowed to re-enter England. In this instance the Protector appears to have overruled the combined advice of both the clergy and the financiers of the City of London, and the Jews were permitted to re-enter England on his personal guarantee.[26] It is clear during the Protectorate that Goodwin maintained lodgings at Whitehall,[27] and the respect of the Protector for the President of Magdalen is indicated by Oliver's suggestion in 1657 through his secretary, John Thurloe, that Henry Cromwell should earmark a certain amount of money from the income of Irish church-lands for Dr. Goodwin's use in preparing and publishing his scholarly works.[28]

In the following year Goodwin and Owen were prime movers in persuading the Protector to sponsor a conference at the Savoy which would enable the Congregational Churches in England to set down a statement of their Faith and polity. The conference of Congregational delegates was convened in the Savoy Palace in the late autumn of that year, although Cromwell died on September 3rd before it commenced. Thomas Goodwin was present and was one of those who ministered to the Lord Protector on his deathbed.[29]

---

[24] *History and Antiquities of Oxford* (edited by John Gutch, 1788–96), II: 661.

[25] Also Ralph Cudworth, Henry Jessey, William Manton, and (apparently) Joseph Caryl. It is interesting to note that of this group Cudworth was a latitudinarian Puritan with Arminian leanings (one of the Cambridge Platonists), Jessey was a Baptist and Manton a Presbyterian. But Goodwin, Owen, Nye and Caryl were all professed Independents — a significant indication of their influence and of Cromwell's confidence.

[26] They had been excluded in 1290, and Cromwell allowed them to return in 1656.

[27] Cf. Abbott, *Writings and Speeches of Oliver Cromwell,* IV : 432.

[28] *Ibid.,* pp. 640, 644.

[29] John Tillotson, later Archbishop of Canterbury, says that he visited Whitehall during the last days of the Protector, and that the Protector was attended by six ministers, among whom were Thomas Goodwin, John Owen, Peter Sterry and Joseph Caryl. He says that " Dr. Goodwin, who had pretended to assure them in a prayer, a very few minutes before he (Cromwell) expir'd,

At the Restoration he did not conform to the episcopal establishment, and he was deprived of the Presidency of Magdalen. He returned to London to minister to an Independent church, and it is said that he lost a half of his considerable library in the Great Fire. He continued his ministry under the trials of the Clarendon Code and the social stigma of Nonconformity until his death at the age of eighty. But although he had known what it was to suffer for his beliefs and suffered some eclipse at the end of his life, in comparison with many of his colleagues Dr. Thomas Goodwin must be counted among the fortunate.

We know something of his foibles. Apparently, he preached regularly at St. Mary's in a velvet cassock, and successive student generations — with the affectionate disrespect that is normal to them — dubbed him " Dr. Nine Caps." It may be that the nickname arose from his custom of wearing two double skullcaps (shown in his portrait),[30] but in view of the carefully itemized and somewhat prolix style of his theological writing, it is not impossible that it also had other connotations for his students. At the same time, he was doubtless one of the ablest men both as scholar and as statesman among the group of Independents, and from all that we know of his dealings with others, he stands out pre-eminently in his commitment to the pastoral vocation of the Christian teacher.

Philip Nye (1596?–1672)

Philip Nye is an enigma. Although he was universally recognized as the political leader of the Independent ministers in the Assembly and became one of the most influential ministers during the Protectorate,[31] his figure remains more or less in the shadows.

---

that he would not die, had now the assurance to say to God, ' Thou hast deceived us, and we were deceived.' " Tillotson was also a witness to Peter Sterry's prayer on the same occasion, Thomas Birch, *The Life of the Most Reverend Dr. John Tillotson* (London, 1752), p. 16.

[30] Suggested by Alexander Gordon in the *D.N.B.*

[31] Clarendon recognized that Nye was one of the " powerful clergy " on the parliamentary side (*History of the Great Rebellion*, VII: 135), Baillie already recognized him as " the head of the independents " in July, 1643 (*Letters and Journals*, II: 81), and Richard Baxter constantly treated him as such in his negotiations to conclude a church settlement between Presbyterians, Independents and Episcopalians (*Reliquiae Baxterianae*, edited by Matthew Sylvester, 1696, Pt. II: 188–93.)

If he was less erudite than Thomas Goodwin, he was an able enough scholar and far more of a practical politician, and this undoubtedly accounts for the widespread reputation he had as a schemer among those who distrusted the Independents. Richard Baxter spoke of " Mr. Phillip Nye's Policie " in the Assembly,[32] Thomas Edwards accused him of playing the politician,[33] while Anthony Wood, who detested him, described him as " a most dangerous and seditious person, a politic Pulpit driver of Independency."[34]

Nye was one of the few ministers of extreme Puritan views to have been educated at Oxford. After coming down from the university, his views seem to have been fairly moderate, for he held charges in the established Church, first as curate at All Hallows, Staining, and then at St. Michael's, Cornhill. Very soon after the fateful meeting with John Cotton in London in 1633, Nye crossed the North Sea to Holland and became minister of a small church of exiles at Arnheim, where he was eventually joined by Thomas Goodwin.

Thomas Edwards, whom we must remember was Independency's most persistent detractor, was nevertheless singularly well-informed about the course of events during the exile. He indicates that the Arnheim congregation was not without its own internal troubles under Nye and Goodwin.[35] It was apparently the claim of the Congregationalists at this time that all their churchly actions had specific authority from the New Testament,[36] and we know that the same principle led the Arnheim congregation to introduce experiments into their worship and discipline which Edwards regarded as dangerously novel. He mentions that the Apologists believed in the weekly celebration of the Lord's Supper,[37] and accused Nye and Goodwin of introducing the " kiss of peace,"[38] the anointing of those who were sick,[39] and the regular use of hymns ![40]

---

[32] *Reliquiae Baxterianae*, Pt. I : 103.
[33] *Antapologia* (1644), p. 217, cf. *Ibid.*, pp. 223, 243.
[34] *Athenae Oxon.*, II : 504.
[35] *Antapologia*, p. 35–38.
[36] *Ibid.*, p. 83.
[37] *Ibid.*, p. 64.
[38] *Ibid.*, p. 60.
[39] *Ibid.*, pp. 36, 59.
[40] *Ibid.*, pp. 59, 294, cf. p. 36.

As the storm clouds of civil war began to gather, Philip Nye returned to England in 1640, and became pastor of a Congregational church at Hull, but at this stage of his career his views on the church did not appear sufficiently distinctive to make him unacceptable to the Presbyterians. If he did not dissemble his real views, he deliberately minimized his differences with the Presbyterian system, probably in the quite genuine hope that he could reconcile the emerging two wings of Puritanism. In view of his later position, it is certainly surprising that very soon after his arrival in Hull he was presented to the living of Kimbolton, Huntingdonshire, by no less a person than Edward Montagu, who later, as the Earl of Manchester, was to be the chief presbyterian protagonist in the Army and in Parliament against Cromwell and the Independents.[41] His connections with some of the leaders on the parliamentary side were responsible for Nye's nomination to the Westminster Assembly as a representative of Huntingdonshire, and he is reputed to have had some influence in the selection of those who were asked to serve[42] — which may account for the fact that almost all those who had served as ministers in the associated congregations of Arnheim and Rotterdam found seats in the Assembly.[43] Meanwhile, while he was at Hull Nye seems already to have been active for the Congregational interest in Yorkshire.[44]

Whatever his views on the Church, there are signs that he very quickly found his mark in the political affairs of the nation. As we have seen, the summer of 1643 had been a grim time for the parliamentary cause, and it had been in this situation that the parliament looked for help from the Scots and dispatched its commissioners, headed by Sir Henry Vane, the younger. Under the leadership of Vane (the youthful governor of Massachusetts at the time of the

---

[41] He had received the courtesy titles " Viscount Mandeville and Baron Kimbolton " when his father became Earl of Manchester in 1626. He acceded to the earldom on the death of his father in 1642.

[42] Alexander Gordon, citing Edmund Calamy, in the *D.N.B.*

[43] Goodwin had been with him in Arnheim, and Simpson, Bridge, and Burroughes had all been associated with the Church at Rotterdam. One exception was Hugh Peter, who was not nominated to the Assembly, and who had been minister at Rotterdam before going to New England at the same time as Henry Vane. Cf. *infra* pp. 110ff.

[44] Edwards, *Antapologia*, p. 217.

controversy with Anne Hutchinson in 1636) with Nye at his elbow, the political interests of the Independents were in very good hands, and it is clear that the Independents were exercising in the State an influence out of all proportion to their numerical weakness.

Even before he arrived in Scotland Nye had been recognized by Robert Baillie as the leader of the Independents. How far this prejudiced Baillie against the sermon Nye preached in Gray Friars Church, Edinburgh, would be difficult to say, but he commented that " Mr. Nye did not please," and went on to add that " His voice was clamorous . . . without grace, . . . without Christ." Baillie conceded, however, that those who heard Nye on the following Sunday said that he " amended it somewhat."[45]

There had been extremely hard bargaining before the *Solemn League and Covenant* was signed, and the loophole left for the Independents to win religious toleration for themselves and others was small enough,[46] but Philip Nye used all his gifts in Scotland and, when he returned, in England to commend the alliance. Wood comments with his habitual animus against Nye, that he " made some Observations from the Pulpit touching the said *Covenant,* shewing the warrant of it from Scripture, and was about that time rewarded for his good Sevice [sic] with the Rectory of *Acton* near London,* in the place of Dr. *Dan. Featley* ejected."[47] Wood never lost the chance of discrediting Philip Nye's motives.

It may have been Nye's early association with Edward Montagu, together with his assiduous advocacy of the *Solemn League and Covenant,* which led Anthony Wood into the error of thinking that up to this time Nye was " a great Champion of the Presbyterian Cause " and only later joined himself to the rising star of Inde-

---

[45] *Letters and Journals,* II : 97. Nye preached in the afternoon of Sunday, August 20th.

[46] Cf. *supra* p. 72.

[47] *Athenae Oxon.,* II : 503. Dr. Featley had been sequestered from both his livings, at Acton and Lambeth, at the same time, on the charge that he was a royalist spy. He compounded in 1645, but the Committee of Plundered Ministers ordered that Nye should be continued at Acton. On the death of Featley in 1645, the Committee put pressure on Bishop Juxon, the patron of the living, to retain the services of Philip Nye. Cf. A. G. Matthews, *Walker Revised: Being a revision of John Walker's Sufferings of the Clergy during the Grand Rebellion 1642–60* (Oxford, Clarendon Press, 1948), p. 47.

pendency.[48] As we have seen, nothing could have been further from the truth, and Philip Nye had already had a good deal to do with putting the star of Independency into the ascendant. In the Assembly, once it became clear that they would not be able to persuade the majority of the members to their views, the efforts of the Independents were directed to prevent the hasty establishment of presbyterian uniformity, and to allow time for their colleagues in Parliament to choose the opportunity to demand toleration from the Houses at Westminster.

Nye's influence with members of his own party is shown by the attempts of the royalists to secure his cooperation. In December 1643 he was offered a royal chaplaincy if he would persuade his colleagues to accept toleration within a moderate episcopacy, and early in the following year Sir Thomas Ogle tried to win him and other leading Independents to the King's cause. But Nye, apart from any question of principle, was far too astute a politician to put much faith in such offers. The leaders of the Independent party realized that their best chance of toleration was to gain control of the Parliamentary party and see that the principle was written into the peace settlement.

During the course of the Civil War, Nye was often used in responsible ecclesiastical and political functions, apart from his leadership of the Independents in the Assembly. In 1646 he was appointed a member of the Committee for sending ministers into Northern parts, and in December 1647 he was one of the commissioners appointed to treat with Charles I in the Isle of Wight. He was one of the ministers who offered his services (declined) to Charles on the morning of the King's execution (January 30th, 1649), and in April the same year he was employed to try to persuade the excluded Members of Parliament to resume their seats. His rapid rise to power and favor under Cromwell parallels that of his colleague, Thomas Goodwin, but Nye did not covet academic preferment, choosing rather to remain in London, close to the seat of government and power. He was appointed a " Trier " in 1654 and an " Ejector " for Middlesex in the same year, and in addition to the rectory at Acton he held four lectureships in London, one of which was held regularly in Westminster Abbey. In view of his

---

[48] *Athenae Oxon.,* II: 503.

many duties at Westminster he secured the assistance of William Clifford at Acton.

In 1654 a group of divines were nominated to define the "Fundamentals of Religion," which were to provide the basis of the religious settlement under the terms of the *Instrument of Government*. Richard Baxter gives us some idea of what went on in that committee, and how some of the less felicitous ideas of John Owen were put under scrutiny by Baxter. Baxter wanted the Creed, the Lord's Prayer and the Decalogue to be the basis of the "Fundamentals," while Owen and his colleagues wanted the essence of Christian doctrine to be set down in more specific terms. Baxter's account continues:

> But the Brethren resolved that they would hold on the way which they had begun: And though they were honest and competently judicious Men, yet those that managed the Business, did want the Judgment and Accurateness which such a Work required, (though they would think any Man supercilious that should tell them so) : And the tincture of Faction stuck so upon their Minds, that it hindered their Judgment. The great doer of all that worded the Articles was Dr. *Owen:* Mr. *Nye,* and Dr. *Goodwin* and Mr. *Syd. Sympson* were his Assistants; and Dr. *Cheynell* his Scribe : Mr. *Marshall* (a sober worthy Man) did something : the rest (sober Orthodox Men) said little, but suffered the Heat of the rest to carry all.[49]

From Baxter's account, his plea that the "Fundamentals" of Christianity should not be too precisely formulated in new standards of orthodoxy sounds closer to Congregational principle than does the position taken by Owen and his colleagues, but we must remember the dangers that the Protectorate faced from the heterodox sects at this time. The importance of the passage is that it clearly shows the pre-eminence of these ministers in the ecclesiastical affairs of the Protectorate. This incident took place over ten years after the *Apologeticall Narration* saw light of day, but Nye, Goodwin and Simpson were no longer representatives of an insignificant minority dancing on a tightrope to win toleration. Through the victories of Cromwell they now had a considerable part in calling the tune.

During the rest of the Protectorate Philip Nye maintained his position. In 1654 he moved from Acton to St. Bartholomew, Ex-

---

[49] *Reliquiae Baxterianae,* Pt. II : 198–99.

change, and he was one of the leaders at the conference of Independent ministers and messengers held at the Savoy Palace in 1658. A curious incident illustrates his influence during the last years of the Protectorate. One day in Whitehall the Lord Protector met Marchamont Needham, the editor of the popular newssheet, *Mercurius Politicus,* and he asked the editor what the latest news was. The editor drily remarked that *vox populi* was saying that Mr. Nye should be Archbishop of Canterbury and Dr. Owen Archbishop of York.[50] It was probably an oblique comment on the fact that in form the Protector's government had almost turned full circle, but it is equally a testimony to the influence which these men were thought to exert.

At the same time neither Owen or Nye supported the move to make Oliver king, and after the death of the Protector Oliver in 1658, Owen seems to have joined with those who were responsible for the overthrow of his son, Richard Cromwell.[51] Many thought that Nye was also involved, but he denied that he had any hand in the dangerous course taken by some of the army officers.[52]

However, his involvement in the policies of Oliver Cromwell was undoubtedly the main reason why he barely escaped exclusion for life from the Act of Oblivion at the Restoration. Even although he escaped the fate of Hugh Peter, he was expressly forbidden on pain of his life from taking any public office in the future[53] — which led Anthony Wood to comment acidly (when someone remarked that Nye was becoming more moderate) that " good reason he had to be, because he was altogether incapacitated from being otherwise."[54] Nye seems to have resigned from his living and public lectureships by the time that Charles II returned. He was licensed as a Congregationalist minister, signed the declaration of other Independent ministers against the rising of the Fifth

---

[50] Robinson to Williamson, March 19, *Cal. S. P. Dom.* (1656–57), p. 318.

[51] *Rel. Baxt.,* Pt. I: 101.

[52] *Ibid.,* pp. 101–102.

[53] " At length it came to his result, that *if* Philip Nye, *Clerk, should after the first of* September *in the Same Year accept or exercise any Office Ecclesiastical, Civil, or Military, he should to all intents and purposes in Law stand as if he had* been totally excepted from life." *Athenae Oxon.,* II: 503.

[54] *Ibid.,* p. 505.

Monarchist, Venner, in 1661, and was one of the deputation of Congregationalists who waited on the King to thank him for the ill-fated Declaration of Indulgence of December 1662. He left London, but returned after the Great Fire of 1666 and was Teacher of the Congregational church which met in Cutlers' Hall, Cloak Lane, of which John Loder was the pastor. He died in Kensington in September 1672.

Although he wrote a defense of his own actions during the Interregnum,[55] he did not leave many writings. He joined with others, however, in writing some extremely able short statements — the introductions written for John Cotton's *Keyes of the Kingdom,* John Norton's *Responsio,* and the *Westminster Directory.* His importance to us is in his leadership in the Westminster Assembly and the fact that he and Thomas Goodwin are thought to have had the major responsibility in writing the *Apologeticall Narration.*[56]

His biographer in the *Dictionary of National Biography,* Alexander Gordon, regarded him, together with John Goodwin and Peter Sterry, as one of the most original minds among the Independents, and observed that " His literary remains, ephemeral pamphlets, are suggestive of the subtle powers which impressed his contemporaries . . . But he had no vulgar ambitions; he sought no personal popularity; the accusation of enriching himself is groundless."[57] Philip Nye was an ecclesiastical statesman, and he was extremely able. At worst he exercised the same kind of duplicity (but with more ability) as those ranged against him; at best he practised a political realism without which the principle of religious toleration might have been swept from seventeenth-century England. He liked to be at the center of direction and effective power, and perhaps it was the ability which he exercised, together with his readiness to stay in the shadows while remaining at

---

[55] *The case of Philip Nye, minister, humbly tendered to the consideration of the parliament* (1662).

[56] Wood, *Athenae Oxon.,* II : 504.

[57] *D.N.B. ad loc.* But cf. Wood's accusations against Nye : Nye " was appointed one of the Triers, or rather *Spanish* Inquisition, for the Approbation of public Preachers; in which Office he acted the Politician so much, that he did not only get his son to be Clerk to them, but also enriched himself with bribes, underhand dealing, and with a living of 400 1. [£] per an, by the help of the said Marshall, one of that number." *Athenae Oxon.,* II : 503.

the center, which caused him to be so much feared and disliked outside the ranks of his own party.

Sidrach Simpson (1600?–1665) and William Bridge (1600?–1670/1)

During the first few decades of the seventeenth century Puritanism bound men together in a fairly close-knit community, particularly in the universities, and Thomas Edwards gives us a hint that he, Thomas Goodwin and William Bridge may have been at Cambridge together and undergone the same influences towards religious conversion.[58] This kind of relationship in their formative years may have laid the foundation of the later association between Sidrach Simpson [or Sympson] and William Bridge. They were much the same age, and both entered Emmanuel College, Cambridge, Simpson being admitted in 1616 and Bridge three years later. However, Simpson seems to have graduated only one year ahead of Bridge (1621–22, 1622–23),[59] and it is reasonable to suppose that they knew each other before they went down from the university.

William Bridge was a Cambridgeshire man, and having proceeded to his Master's degree in 1626, he was elected to a fellowship in his college. During the years 1631–36 he was occupied in various lectureships in Essex and Norfolk, the last being at St. Peters Hungate where his Puritanism was called in question as a result of Archbishop Laud's Visitation to those parts in 1635. His opposition to the prevailing government in the national Church was so clear that he was deprived in 1636 by Matthew Wren, Bishop of Norwich and Laud's most effective and persistent agent in the eastern fenlands,[60] and a writ *de excommunicato capiendo* was

---

[58] *Antapologia*, pp. 95–96. Edwards was born in 1599, and was in Cambridge (Queens College) at the same time as some of the Apologists.

[59] John Venn and J. A. Venn, (Ed.), *The Book of Matriculations and Degrees, ... in the University of Cambridge from 1544 to 1659* (Cambridge Univ. Press), *ad loc.*

[60] Wren knew the Cambridge situation and had been Master of Peterhouse. As a rigorous exponent of the royal prerogative and something of a liturgist, he was a willing supporter of the Laudian policy. He had been appointed Bishop of Hereford in 1634, but was translated to Norwich in the following year. In 1638 he was translated to the see of Ely, and carried out a Visitation of the Ely diocese that resulted in a determined attack on the Puritanism in that district.

issued against him.[61] Bridge therefore migrated to Holland together with some wealthy families, and joined himself to the gathered church in Rotterdam, where Samuel Ward, formerly of Ipswich in Suffolk, was pastor.[62] It seems that with this background of recent history, Bridge renounced his previous ordination in the Episcopal Church of England and was re-ordained as Teacher according to the Congregational pattern by Samuel Ward and the church at Rotterdam.[63]

Meanwhile, after leaving the university, Sidrach Simpson went to a curacy at St. Margaret's, Fish Street, in London, where he also held a lectureship and made a name for himself in the City as a preacher. However, he too was called to account as a result of Laud's Metropolitan Visitation, and at first made his submission, but in 1638 migrated to Holland and joined himself to the same church at Rotterdam.

For the events that followed during the somewhat disturbed years in this congregation we have a very full account in Thomas Edwards's *Antapologia*.[64] Edwards was extremely virulent against the Independents, and that would make his account suspect; but he appears to have been extremely well acquainted with the facts, having based his account upon information supplied by William Bridge himself and upon the written letters of Simpson and others who were involved in the controversy. Therefore, however much of his interpretation may be open to question, we must accept the fact that the events took place, and possibly very much in the order and way that he describes them. It is typical of Edwards that he had not the least compunction in using the information supplied by Bridge to blacken not only the reputation of the Independents generally, but also that of his own chief informant.

Soon after Simpson's arrival at Rotterdam he began to take exception to some of the procedures in the church. In particular,

---

[61] Neal, *History of the Puritans,* III : 174.

[62] *Antapologia*, pp. 35, 57, 142. Care must be taken to distinguish Samuel Ward of Ipswich from another of the same name, the third Master of Sidney Sussex College. There are no less than eight " Samuel Wards " listed in Venn's *Book of Matriculations and Degrees* between the years 1588 and 1659.

[63] Matthews, *Calamy Revised, ad loc.*

[64] *Antapologia,* pp. 35, 142ff.

Edwards records, " he stood for the ordinance of prophesying to be exercised in that Church, that the people on the Lords dayes should have liberty after the Sermons ended, to put doubts and questions to the Ministers, &c. and he was troubled at a ruling Elder in that Church brought in by Mr *Bridge* (which belike had more power and bore more sway than himselfe)."[65] As a result of this difference, Simpson left the church without waiting for letters of dismission, and with the help of a certain Mrs. White, founded a new church, which at the beginning had five members.[66] Samuel Ward sympathized with those who had left on the question of " prophesying "[i.e., preaching], and the upshot of his disagreement with Bridge was that for this and other reasons (none of them substantial) he was deposed from his position as pastor.

Meanwhile the right of the private member to prophesy was regarded as a matter of importance in Simpson's church, and acceptance of this principle seems to have been required of those who applied for membership.[67] But the schismatic congregation grew apace by defections from Bridge's followers, and the bitterness of the dispute grew to the point where Bridge admitted that " there were no such sharpe tongues or bitter divisions as these." Simpson also carried on an extensive correspondence with their mutual friends in England, and more fuel was added to the fire by the letters that Bridge and Ward wrote against each other. In his account Edwards somewhat takes the side of his informant, William Bridge, and claims that the scandals had been the prime cause of Mrs. Bridge's premature death.[68] Jeremiah Burroughes took Ward's place in the original congregation (as Teacher), but the former returned to England in 1641, and Samuel Ward was reinstated as a result of the council described in the *Apologeticall Nar-*

---

[65] *Ibid.,* p. 142.

[66] *Ibid.,* pp. 35, 142. It should be remembered that Simpson was at this time only a member of the congregation. His insistence on the private members' right of " prophesying " *may* at least be partially understood in terms of a preacher who had perforce to listen rather than exercise his art!

[67] *Ibid.,* p. 96.

[68] *Ibid.,* p. 144. Bridge married twice. His first wife was Susannah, and his second wife was Margaret the widow of John Arnold. Cf. Matthews, *Calamy Revised, ad loc.*

ration (p. 20f.). The whole unhappy incident was terminated by the change of conditions in England which enabled the exiles to return home.

Although the dispute between Simpson and Bridge had been deep and acrimonious it did not affect their readiness to work together for the good of their cause. On his return in 1641, Simpson lectured again at St. Margaret, Fish Street, and at Blackfriars. Against the Apologists' claim that they had refrained from advocating their views by preaching,[69] Edwards claimed that they were all very active in the Congregational interest. " Mr *Simpson,* (one of the Apologists,) hath frequently, and did constantly (for one space) in many Lectures at *Black-friers* . . . preach for his opinions and way, and did answer many objections against their Church-way, pleading strongly for it, and for pretended Liberty of conscience and toleration : So on *Fishstreet-hill,* on that Text of *Rom.* 12.2 . . . he preached largely for his Church-way, and propounded and resolved nine Questions about it : And at *Westminster* also, in Sermons preached there, he had many passages for the Church-way, as for Toleration, as for the matter of their Church, visible Saints, &c."[70] Sidrach Simpson's actions in Holland may have made him appear more as a Schismatic Separatist than as an adherent of the Congregational Way, but within the Westminster Assembly and in his public advocacy of the common cause he did not hesitate to join himself to the other Dissenting brethren, nor do they appear to have had any hesitation in counting him as a colleague. This fact needs to be set against the picture painted by Edwards.

In 1644 Simpson defended their views in print by publishing *The Anatomist Anatomized,* which was a reply to Alexander Forbes's attack, *The Anatomie of Independencie.* He signed the *Apologeticall Narration* and the *Reasons* they submitted against Presbyterian government in 1645,[71] and the confidence of the Independent party in him is indicated by his nomination by the Visitors to Cambridge University in 1650 to the Mastership of Pembroke Hall.

---

[69] Cf. *Apologeticall Narration,* p. 25f.

[70] *Op. cit.,* pp. 215–16.

[71] *The Reasons of the Dissenting Brethren against the Third Proposition, concerning Presbyterial Government.*

About the same time he obtained the living of St. Mary Abchurch in London, where he organized the parish after the Congregational pattern, and in 1652 with Owen, Goodwin, Caryl, Lockyer, Peter and others he was in a conference with Cromwell about providing ministerial salaries for service in Ireland.[72] The confidence continued, for in 1653 he became rector of St. Bartholomew, Exchange, preached the Cambridge Commencement sermon, and was appointed a " Trier " in the following year. Whatever the difficulties had been in Holland, since his return Simpson had proved himself to be in complete agreement with his colleagues in the Westminster Assembly (or they with him) and loyal to the Independent government in Church and State. However, illness may have affected his disposition in his closing years, and he seems to have been in disfavor for preaching against Cromwell's government. He died in 1655.[73]

Whether it was the result of wisdom or of Providence we do not know, but on his return to England William Bridge decided to avoid the capital and leave it to his erstwhile colleague and recent " thorn in the flesh," Sidrach Simpson. Bridge went first to Norwich, but very soon settled in Yarmouth and, as a result of his ministrations, in 1642 he is credited with having founded Congregational churches in both these towns which have had a continuous history to the present day.[74]

---

[72] Abbott, *Writings and Speeches of Oliver Cromwell*, II : 568 note.

[73] *D.N.B. ad loc.*

[74] Old Meeting, Norwich, and Middlegate, Great Yarmouth. During the Interregnum these gathered churches met in the parish churches, but this was not possible after the Restoration. The meetinghouse of Old Meeting dates from 1693 after the passing of the Toleration Act, and the following Covenant, which was formulated under the ministry of Bridge is still in force :

" We, whose names are underwritten, being desirous in the fear of God, to worship and serve Him, according to His revealed will, do freely, solemnly, and jointly covenant with the Lord, in the presence of His saints and angels.

1. That we will for ever acknowledge and avouch God for our God in Jesus Christ.

2. That we will always endeavour through the Grace of God assisting us, to walk in all His ways and ordinances, according to His written Word, which is the only sufficient rule of good life for every man; neither will we suffer ourselves to be polluted by any sinful ways, either public or private, but abstain from the very appearance of evil, giving no offence to the Jew or Gentile, or Churches of Christ.

Bridge was also known as a preacher in London, and he was a popular preacher before Parliament and in the city during the course of his attendances at the sessions of the Assembly. Edwards described one sermon by Bridge in which Bridge had represented the people of a congregation as " Gods porters to let the Ministers into the Church, and how no men come in truly called but they." This obviously implied the Congregational view of what constituted a valid ordination and ministry. Bridge felt most free to advocate the Congregational Way while preaching in the counties of East Anglia: " In the Countrey too, he hath preached for his way (as I have been enformed by a good hand,) both at *Norwich,* and at *Ipswich,"* and although Edwards as yet had no information about Bridge's behavior at Yarmouth, he was prepared to believe the worst and promised to present the evidence in a later book.[75] Bridge knew and belonged to the eastern counties which were the stronghold of Puritanism: he sat in the Assembly as a representative of Norfolk, and it was to that county that he gave his real ministry.

Bridge had been Edwards's informant about the proceedings at Rotterdam, and for that reason Edwards may have been slightly more conciliatory towards him than towards some of the other Apologists; but there is also evidence that Bridge was more sympathetic to Presbyterian views than were some of his colleagues,

---

3. That we will in all love, improve our Communion as brethren, by watching over one another, and as need shall be, counsel, admonish, reprove, comfort, relieve, assist, and bear with one another, humbly submitting ourselves to the government of Christ in His churches.

4. Lastly, we do not promise these things in our own, but in Christ's strength; neither do we confine ourselves to the words of this Covenant, but shall at all times account it our duty to embrace any further light on truth, which shall be revealed to us out of God's Word."

This was signed on behalf of the Church on June 28th, 1643, by:

William Bridge	Samuel Alexander
Christopher Steygold	James Gedny
William Starfe	William Officiall
Francis Olley	John Balderstone
John Leverington	Samuel Clarke

John Eyre

The Covenant was re-affirmed in June, 1932.

[75] *Antapologia,* p. 216.

for he and Edwards were equally opposed to members of the congregation "prophesying." Furthermore, at Yarmouth William Bridge lived on very good terms with a Presbyterian minister, John Brinsley, the younger, and championed him against those who were trying to exclude him from his charge.[76]

In 1646 Bridge took the lectureship at Stepney, London, possibly in the place of his old friend and colleague, Jeremiah Burroughes, who died in that year. He was made an assistant to the Commission for Norfolk in 1654, and attended the conference at the Savoy in 1658, but he appears to have taken no prominent part in national affairs after the death of Cromwell. He remained in his position as town preacher at Yarmouth until he was ejected at the Restoration — a post which he had held since 1642. He moved to London and lived at Clapham, a western suburb of seventeenth-century London in the county of Surrey, and he may even have been responsible for founding the Congregational church in that place. While in London he narrowly escaped being captured while attending a nonconformist conventicle, but in 1666 he returned to Yarmouth and began to preach again with the connivance of the borough corporation. However, he was ultimately summoned to the sessions at Norwich in 1669 and forbidden to preach under the terms of the Five Mile Act within the county of Norfolk. He therefore went to the next county, Suffolk, and preached there. He died in March 1670/1.[77]

William Bridge possessed a good library, and he has been described as "a hard student, and rose every morning winter and summer at four of the clock"[78] — and to do that consistently in a parish on the Norfolk coast needs stamina! He was a popular preacher with an unrivaled reputation in Norfolk. He made no attempt to influence the higher reaches of national affairs, but his opinion carried great weight in his own adopted county and throughout the fen country.[79] If he shared some views with Pres-

---

[76] Cf. Matthews, *Calamy Revised, ad loc.*

[77] *Ibid.* A. G. Matthews has added a good deal to the article on Bridge by J. H. Thorpe in the *D.N.B.* Thorpe says that Bridge died at Clapham, but Neal in his *History of the Puritans* gives Yarmouth as the place of his death; *op. cit.,* III: 174.

[78] Neal, *op. cit.,* III: 174.

[79] Cf. *Ibid.,* note.

byterians, there can be no doubt about his fidelity to the Congregational Way, and not the least of his achievements is the fact that he was personally responsible for the establishment of two, if not three, Congregational churches that have enjoyed continuous life to the present day.

Jeremiah Burroughes (1599–1646)

It is appropriate at the end of a chapter which has inevitably relied a good deal upon the biased testimony of Thomas Edwards that we should turn to Jeremiah Burroughes, for in his *Vindication*[80] and *Irenicum*[81] he did more than any other to meet Edwards's slanders and calumnies.

From the point of view of background and training no man was more typical of the Puritanism about which we are writing. Born in 1599 he was of much the same age as Thomas Goodwin, Bridge and Simpson, and entered Emmanuel College, Cambridge, within a year of Simpson (1617). He was almost inevitably drawn into the little circle of radical Puritans which found its center in that college — indeed, Edwards hints that the Apologists had been close friends for some time.[82]

Neal says that Burroughes was obliged to leave the university for his Puritanism.[83] He went first to assist Edmund Calamy, the elder, at Bury St. Edmunds, in Suffolk, and then (1631) accepted the living at Tivetshall in Norfolk, but in 1636 he too fell under suspension for his attitude to Bishop Wren's Injunctions, and for refusal to read the Book of Sports. He was offered hospitality by the Earl of Warwick, a Puritan peer who was a great supporter of the harassed Puritan clergy.

Thomas Edwards gives us the impression that when Ward was deposed from the Rotterdam congregation, Burroughes simply stepped into his place; but in his *Vindication* Jeremiah Burroughes corrects that impression. He says that while he was with Lord

---

[80] *A Vindication of Mr. Burroughes, Against Mr. Edwards his foule Aspersions in his spreading Gangraena, and his angry Antiapologia. Concluding with a brief Declaration what the Independents would have* (1644).

[81] *Irenicum, to the Lovers of Truth and Peace. Heart-Divisions opened In the Causes and Evils of them* (1646).

[82] *Antapologia*, p. 13f.

[83] *History of the Puritans*, II : 427.

Warwick he received his first approach from the church at Rotterdam "to joyn with Mr. Bridge in the worke of the Lord in that church."[84] He must have declined because the deputation returned to Holland without him. Very soon after this, however, the ecclesiastical pressure upon him at home was increased, for he heard that he was to be accused of certain ecclesiastical offenses, and being unwilling to be an embarrassment to his host he went up to London to meet the charges. He appeared to have allayed the suspicion of the authorities, but he discovered that the charges were renewed as soon as he left the capital. Edwards also suggests — and there is no reason to doubt it — that he was in trouble with the government for certain outspoken comments he had made regarding the Scottish war.[85]

By this time the Earl of Warwick had fallen ill, and Burroughes was in a real quandary about his future. He did not wish to encroach further upon Lord Warwick's hospitality, but it was clear that he could not expect any place or preferment in the English Church. Therefore, when the church at Rotterdam renewed its invitation with a definite call to become its Teacher, he could not but regard this as providential; and these were the circumstances in which he accepted their offer and crossed to join the other exiles in Holland.

He does not seem to have taken any active part in the dissensions at Rotterdam, but eventually returned to England in 1641 and became Lecturer at Stepney. Burroughes lectured regularly at 7 A.M. and William Greenhill gave the evening lecture in the same parish — a fact which caused Hugh Peter to dub them "the Morning and Evening Stars of Stepney."[86] Burroughes was also Lecturer later in the day at Cripplegate. He did not, however, take a regular living in the Church or attempt to gather a congregation of his own,[87] and this caused Richard Baxter to infer that Burroughes was rather less of a convinced Congregationalist than the other Dissenting Brethren, for Baxter observes that as "he never practised their Church-gathering way, so at last he was contented

---

[84] *Vindication*, p. 19.
[85] *Antapologia*, p. 19.
[86] *Athenae Oxon.*, II: 606.
[87] Neal, *History of the Puritans*, II: 427.

to have united on the Terms which were offered."[88] This is at variance with Burroughes's clear statement of his position in the *Irenicum* and in a speech which he delivered about the time that the establishment of Presbyterianism was being voted by Parliament,[89] and it should be remembered that if Burroughes did not gather a church when he returned to England neither did he re-enter the parochial system. A far more practical reason seems more likely to have governed Burroughes's concentration upon Sunday lectureships during the course of the Assembly, namely, the need to remain in London, and to have employment which would leave him free to attend the Assembly's sessions.[90]

However, Burroughes does represent to some extent the right-wing of the Independent position. Edwards recognized that Burroughes and Bridge represented the non-separatist Congregationalism of the New England way,[91] and both men were judged to be conformable moderates until Bishop Wren's measures overtook them.[92] Jeremiah Burroughes was also regarded by his Presbyterian contemporaries as one of the more conciliatory of the Independents, probably on account of his *Irenicum,* which Baxter described as an " excellent book "[93] and which was published in the year of Burroughes's death. It is a book which reveals that the

---

[88] *Rel. Baxt.,* I : 103.

[89] The establishment of Presbyterianism was voted on March 5th, 1646, and Burroughes, speaking on behalf of the Independents, made his speech on March 9th, Neal, *History of the Puritans,* II : 381. Cf. Gardiner *History of the Great-Civil War* (1893 edition; Longmans, London), III : 76f.

[90] During the course of the Assembly almost all the Independents who were members secured lectureships or livings in or near the capital. Among the Apologists only William Bridge had a charge that was very distant from London, but he appears to have managed to visit the city fairly frequently. But even Bridge took a London lectureship in 1646. Of the other Independents who were members of the Assembly only John Green of Pencombe, Anthony Burgess of Sutton Coldfield (both in the county of Warwick), and John Phillips of Wrentham in Suffolk had charges that tended to keep them in the provinces. It seems reasonable to suppose that the others regarded attendance in the Assembly as such a priority that most of them found means of remaining near the City.

[91] *Antapologia,* p. 11f.

[92] *Ibid.,* p. 17f.

[93] *Rel. Baxt.,* I : 103.

author was willing to go a considerable distance for union with the Presbyterians, but it no less throws into clear relief some of the major differences, particularly in the nature of ministerial authority in the Church.

A joint Committee of Accommodation had been set up by the House of Lords, House of Commons and the Divines of the Assembly to try to discover some way in which the Independent churches might be included within the terms of the Presbyterian settlement, or if not, the terms on which they could be granted toleration. The attempt at comprehension failed because the Presbyterians, with the assistance of the Scots, maneuvered their system through Parliament without waiting for the Independents to present their alternative plan.[94] The Committee for Accommodations was then revived in November 1645 to consider the question of Toleration,[95] but this proved equally objectionable to Presbyterian divines, and at its last meeting on March 9th, 1646, Jeremiah Burroughes was deputed to speak for the Independents against the threat of a new uniformity:

> Hereupon the reverend Mr Jer. Burroughs, a divine of great candour and moderation, declared in the name of the Independents, " that if their congregations might not be exempted from that coercive power of the classes; if they might not have liberty to govern themselves in their own way, as long as they behaved peaceably towards the civil magistrate; they were resolved to suffer or go to some other place of the world, where they might enjoy their liberty. But while men think that there is no way of peace but by forcing all to be of the same mind (says he), while they think the civil sword is an ordinance of God to determine all controversies of divinity, and that it must needs be attended with fines and imprisonment to the disobedient; while they apprehend that there is no medium between a strict uniformity, and a general confusion of all things; while these sentiments prevail, there must be a base subjection of men's consciences to slavery, a suppression of much truth, and great disturbances in the Christian world.[96]

---

94 Neal, *Hist. of the Puritans,* II: 377.

95 The Independent divines on this committee, according to Neal, were the five Apologists and a " Mr. Drury." Since there was no member of the Assembly with that name it was almost certainly John Dury, the great ecumenical figure of that century, who had already undergone both Presbyterian and Episcopal ordination in his attempts to bring the churches together. *Ibid.,* II: 378.

96 *Ibid.,* p. 381.

This speech delivered on March 9th, 1646 was in some ways an epitaph for Jeremiah Burroughes. In the autumn of that year he fell from his horse, and after an illness of two weeks he died (probably from pneumonia) on November 13th.[97] He was regarded with great respect by those who did not share his views on church polity. Richard Baxter recalls him as " that good Man Mr Jeremiah Burroughs," and he used to say that if all Episcopalians had been like Archbishop Ussher, all Presbyterians like Stephen Marshall, and all Independents like Jeremiah Burroughes, the divisions of the Church might readily have been healed.[98] Even Robert Baillie grudgingly set it down on record in 1643 that Burroughes, with Goodwin and Bridge, were " men full, as it yet seems, of grace and modestie."[99]

Like Zwingli, Burroughes suffers from having died too soon in the history of a movement, and his importance among the Dissenting Brethren has tended to be overlooked. Yet the respect in which members of his own party held him is evidenced by the fact that in 1657 they sponsored an ambitious new edition of his major works.[100] However, his death in 1646 is important for another rea-

---

[97] A newssheet, *Perfect Occurrences,* for 13th Nov. 1646 gives the circumstances in which Burroughes met his death, and is cited by John Brown *The History of Congregationalism and Memorials of the Churches in Norfolk and Suffolk* (1877), p. 115; followed by *D. N. B.;* Neal seems to be in error when he says that Burroughes died of a consumptive disease on Nov. 14th, cf. *op. cit.,* II : 427.

[98] Cf. *Ibid.; D.N.B. ad loc.* Baxter's high opinion of Burroughes is certainly seen in *Rel. Baxt.,* I : 103.

[99] *Letters and Journals,* II : 111.

[100] The sponsors were the four who signed the *Apologeticall Narration* with him, together with William Greenhill, his colleague at Stepney, John Yates and William Alderley, and the works were published by Peter Cole, at his printing press at Cornhill, near the Royal Exchange. A perusal of the advertisements of the books offered for sale by this publisher in 1657 is very instructive both as to the popularity of the Puritan writers, and also as to those who could be regarded as falling within roughly the same theological and ecclesiastical wing. Mr. Cole as a good man of business could still find buyers for Laud's sermon at Charles I's coronation and for the speeches of Laud and of the King from the scaffold. He also offered books by those who were certainly not Independents. But by far the biggest features in the advertisement were eleven books of Thomas Hooker's works (in three volumes), carrying a

son, it brought to the fore John Owen, the great systematizer of English Congregationalism and its leading theological figure during the rest of the century. Richard Baxter recalls that " Mr. *Burroughs* being dead, Dr. *John Owen* arose, not of the same Spirit, to fill up his place; by whom and Mr. *Philip Nye's* Policie the Flames were encreased, our Wounds kept open, and carried on as if there had been none but they considerable in the World."[101]

We realize that Baxter and Owen were to engage in many theological jousts during the next few decades, and we may not altogether accept his strictures on the future Dean of Christ Church or his estimate of Owen's effect upon the ecclesiastical situation. But he clearly recognized the leadership that Owen gave to the Congregationalists, and if the place and prestige of John Owen in the ranks of his own party were inherited from Jeremiah Burroughes, it means that the latter was a much more important figure to his contemporaries than we have hitherto suspected.

* * * * *

It is perhaps unnecessary to go into great detail about those who were associated with the five Apologists at Westminster. William Greenhill and William Carter (junior) joined with them in signing the *Reasons,* and we know from John Lightfoot's *Journal*[102] that Carter was one of their most persistent supporters. Joseph Caryl and Peter Sterry were also known to be Independents, and the group seems to have included John Bond, John Green, and

---

commendatory epistle by Thomas Goodwin and Philip Nye, twenty-one books by William Bridge (in two volumes), and twelve books by Jeremiah Burroughes. Also among the offerings in theology, which represent by far the biggest section, there were works by John Rogers of Dedham, Samuel Ward of Ipswich, Peter Sterry, Sidrach Simpson, John Owen, John Goodwin, Nicholas Love, [John?] Phillips, and three treatises (apart from Hooker) out of New England — *The Discipline of the Church in New England,* a tract by John Eliot and T. Mayhew on work among the Indians, and Stone's *A Congregational Church is a Catholick Visible Church.* The details of this advertisement are taken from the 1657 edition of Burroughes's *Gospel Reconciliation: or Christs Trumpet of Peace to the World.*

[101] *Rel. Baxt.,* I: 103.

[102] *The Journal of the Proceedings of the Assembly of Divines, from January 1, 1643, to December 31, 1644,* published as volume XIII of John Lightfoot's *Works* (London, 1824), edited by the Revd. John Rogers Pitman.

(possibly) Anthony Burgess. John Phillips also spoke out at one or two crucial places in the debates, and this is of particular interest since he was the only divine in the Assembly who had experienced exile in New England.[103]

Mention of John Phillips's life in New England introduces an intriguing question about the policy of the Dissenting Brethren in the Assembly. We wonder why, over against all their desire to get literary help from New England, the experiments across the Atlantic played such a little part in the presentation of their case. We know that the New England leaders had been invited to join the Westminster Assembly and that they had declined;[104] but perhaps it had been assumed that they would. Sir Henry Vane had been governor of Massachusetts in the early days of the colony,[105] and yet both he and John Phillips were curiously reticent about their experiences in the Puritan Commonwealth.

The failure to use Hugh Peter in the Assembly is particularly

---

[103] He returned to England in 1642, and Winthrop remarks that unlike some of those who sailed at the same time, Phillips did not run down New England but " spake well of the people, and of the country." Winthrop's *Journal*, II : 83.

[104] Cotton, Davenport and Hooker had been invited, and Hooker dissuaded them from returning to England, but we should note that the reason why he was able to persuade his colleagues not to sail was because of letters that arrived from England from Hugh Peter and Thomas Welde. Cf. Winthrop's *Journal*, II : 71–72.

[105] Vane had arrived in Massachusetts in October 1635, and owing to his personal charm and distinguished birth he had been elected governor (despite the rivalry of John Winthrop) in March 1636, at the age of twenty-four. He was immediately involved in the controversy with Anne Hutchinson, and subsequently in differences with Winthrop. Having been displaced by Winthrop in the elections of 1637, he returned to England in the summer of that year. It is clear from a letter he later wrote to Winthrop that he distinguished between the different situation in which the followers of the Congregational Way found themselves in New England and that which faced them at home (June 10th, 1645), but it seems that even on American soil Vane had been much more disposed towards toleration than was Winthrop. See the letter to Winthrop, reproduced in facsimile in James K. Hosmer's *Young Sir Henry Vane* (Houghton, Mifflin Company, Boston and New York, 1888), pp. 79–81 ; and for the disputes in Boston, *Ibid.*, pp. 60–82. For Winthrop's account of the same events see Winthrop's *Journal*, " *History of New England* " (edited by James Kendall Hosmer, Barnes and Noble, New York, 1959 reprint), I : 182, 195–206, 207–212, 215f. [referred to as Winthrop's *Journal*].

difficult to understand. He had arrived in England during the autumn of 1641 as the agent of the Massachusetts settlers, and after a brief episode as a chaplain with Lord Forbes's expedition to Ireland, he had returned to England before the Assembly opened and had been very active in public affairs. Indeed, in September 1643, at much the same time as the Assembly was getting ready to welcome the Scots, the Committee of Safety had appointed Peter as an envoy to the Dutch.

The omission is the more remarkable when we remember that Peter was probably the only man in England who had had experience of the Congregational experiments in both Holland and New England. It had been Peter who, with no less a person than William Ames, had first organized the church at Rotterdam on a Covenant basis. He had sailed to New England in 1635 with young Henry Vane and, upon landing, at once had taken a full part in the affairs of the colony. He was a " natural " for the Independents in the Assembly.

We can only conclude that Hugh Peter was an embarrassment to them. His want of tact became well known, but perhaps we must look deeper than that. We get a clue to the reason in the part he played during the disputes that had threatened to divide the colony of Massachusetts soon after he and Henry Vane arrived in New England. Vane had been elected Governor in the Spring of 1636 and had tended to side with the religious malcontents against the regular Ministers. He was roundly rebuked by Hugh Peter, who among other things " besought him humbly to consider his youth, and short experience in the things of God, and to beware of peremptory conclusions, which he perceived him to be very apt unto."[106]

I suggest that it was not only the memory of Hugh Peter's effrontery which was the issue, but his support of the religious uniformity which the New England clergy were enforcing, for on this same occasion he had referred very openly to the divisions he had experienced among the churches while he had been in the Netherlands.[107] If the former would still rankle with Vane, the latter might well frighten Nye and his colleagues. When he returned to

---

[106] Winthrop's *Journal,* I : 204.
[107] *Ibid.*

England Hugh Peter was the representative of the New England colonists, and there was no reason to suppose either that he had modified his views or that he intended to remain in England. He actually did both, but this could not be foreseen. Sir Henry Vane was at this time perhaps the most important single man in the English Parliament. He and the Independents were trying to unite all religious sects in opposition to the Presbyterians, and Hugh Peter must have represented a considerable embarrassment to their policy, for they were becoming increasingly conscious that in respect to religious toleration the Congregational Way in England lay in an opposite direction to the path it had taken in New England. The English Independents were more than willing to receive whatever support the New England theologians could give them in defining the positive worship, government and discipline of their doctrine of the Church, but they were not too anxious to have the uniformity of the New England system discussed publicly in the debates of the Assembly — certainly not by anyone as tactless and outspoken as the Reverend Hugh Peter.

The Basic Issue:
"And what further authority?"

U P TO this point we have stressed the relationship between the ecclesiological and the political aspects of the struggle within the parliamentary party, and this has been done deliberately because church historians are apt to be somewhat shy in recognizing that connection. However, it should not be assumed that political aims and methods invalidated the theological motivation of those who debated in the Westminster Assembly, or that those who expressed strong views in the dispute were insincere in their profession of faith. We must rather insist that both those who advocated the acceptance of Scottish Presbyterianism and the adherents of the Congregational Way were very firmly convinced that their own view of the Church was closest to the Scriptural pattern.

The *Apologeticall Narration* begins with an account of the circumstances that had led its authors into nonconformity and exile, and then the writers set out their practices in worship and discipline. They emphasize that in worship, ministry and discipline they follow the same general example of all the Reformed Churches. In the main part of the pamphlet they proceed to establish the principles that had guided their practice: first, the primitive pattern of the Apostolic churches; secondly, the maxim never to make their present judgment binding, lest they should err through " a mis-understanding of the rule "; thirdly, to act in accordance with what most Reformed Churches " did acknowledge warrentable."

It was within this third principle that they introduce — perhaps a little too ingenuously — the things that were most controversial in their practice. They claim that they were following what most Reformed Churches regarded as warrantable in Scripture, even when they advance views which were not accepted by the majority of those churches. As one example they refer to the qualifications they required for membership in the church: they wish to receive into the church only those whom all churches would recognize as belonging to the Body of Christ, although they maintain their willingness to accept " the meanest in whom there may be supposed to be the least of Christ." They also instance their practice of extempore prayer (which all Reformed churches agreed to be lawful), although they insist that they do not condemn those who use liturgical forms. Finally, they claim their church government to be consistent with what all Reformed Christians agree to be true to the New Testament, for all Churches were agreed on the powers of the particular congregation! What they fail to point out is that by concentrating jurisdiction in the local church they actually introduce a very radical modification of the system practiced by most of the Reformed Churches.

They admit it was a sin for an individual congregation to claim an absolute independence from all other congregations, but they question whether an officer in the church should exercise jurisdiction within congregations or towards members to which (or whom) he was bound by no particular pastoral relationship. They do not doubt the importance and usefulness of synods, but they assert the Biblical justification and effectiveness of their own synodical practice, which stops short of allowing the synod the power of excommunication. They cite as evidence their dealings in the schism at Rotterdam.

The last part of the booklet is addressed more particularly to their present situation and the embarrassment caused by the rumors and calumnies of which they complain, and they conclude with a clear plea that Parliament grant them liberty of conscience.

Therefore, if we use the *Apologeticall Narration* as our guide we see that we can review the distinctive features of the Congregational Way under three main heads: worship, polity and discipline, and the underlying principles.

1. *On Worship.*

When Robert Baillie became acquainted with the sacramental practice of the Independents he thought it was " very irreverent ": he apparently disapproved of their weekly celebration of the Lord's

Supper, thought they were lax in not providing adequate prepara-
tion for the sacrament, and disliked the brief prayers and long
silences in the service.[1] Also, we may remember, he had not been
very favorably impressed by Philip Nye's preaching.[2] Presumably, then, there were differences in worship between the Independents and the Presbyterians.

However, these differences were not the fundamental points of
divergence. The Independents might prefer one prayer before the
sermon to the Presbyterians' two, Goodwin might argue strongly
for the service beginning with prayers for the King and those in
Authority,[3] and Philip Nye might hold the private opinion that a
minister's head should be covered during the sermon and uncovered
during the Lord's Supper,[4] but no one imagined that if there had
been no more fundamental questions than these the differences
would have remained irremovable barriers to unity. The Apologists were able to point to the normal form of their services as a
point at which they and their Presbyterian colleagues in the Assembly would be in clear agreement, and although they admitted that
their own normal practice was for extempore prayer, they could
also claim that this was accepted as Scripturally lawful by all.
Indeed, in matters of worship, psalmody and the sacrament the
differences were more pronounced as between Scottish and English usages than they were between Independents and Presbyterians
per se. The point of dissent did not fall within the area of the
Directory of Worship.

2. On Polity.

It is generally assumed on both sides that the fundamental differences between the Congregationalists and the Presbyterians
were in polity. Admittedly, their understanding of the Scriptural
rule and their literalistic interpretations of the New Testament
held implications for polity that were to be illustrated in the history
of these two denominations in England and America within the
following centuries.

On the other hand, their systems of church government were if

---

[1] *Letters and Journals*, II: 148f.
[2] *Ibid.*, p. 97.
[3] *Ibid.*, p. 123.
[4] *Ibid.*, p. 149.

anything more similar than they are today. The Apologists claimed that they "set up no other but the very same which the reformed Churches judge necessary and sufficient, and as instituted by Christ and his Apostles for the perpetuall government of his Church, that is, *Pastors, Teachers, Ruling Elders,* (with us not lay but Ecclesiastique persons separated to that service) and *Deacons.*"[5] In the concept of the ministry and of the spiritual power which a minister exercised there could hardly be any "higher" doctrine than that which was held by Jeremiah Burroughes, for he declared that the members of a church could not limit or control the spiritual powers that were inherent in the ministry, "but once a man be chosen an Officer of the Church, all the power that ever that office had since Christ's time, in any Church in all the Christian world, or ever can have to the coming of Christ againe, falls upon him."[6] But this power was spiritual and not coercive: it was derived from the example of a ministry, and not from the pattern of a Civil State. Behind it there was the example of the One who spoke with authority, but who had refused to use the sword. For this reason, authority within the Church must be exercised with great care, "that when we seek to pluck up tares, we pluck not up wheat also."[7]

The Congregationalists were opposed to a hierarchy of church courts as they were opposed to an episcopal hierarchy, precisely because they believed that authority in the Church is the authority of Jesus Christ. This authority was possessed by the local covenanted congregation as a microcosm of the whole. In their view there could be no higher authority than the authority of Jesus Christ within the local church, although there could be extensions of it within a synod or assembly. However, the local church was the *locus* of Christ's authority because this was the place where the distinct functions of kerygmatic ministry and jurisdiction were held together.

There are some grounds for thinking that because the Independents of the Westminster Assembly were under pressure from the Presbyterian side of the argument they tended to become more

---

[5] *Ibid.*, p. 8.

[6] *Irenicum, to the Lovers of Truth and Peace* (1646), p. 51.

[7] *Ibid.*, p. 58.

" Independent " during the course of the debate, just as there are grounds for thinking that because the New England divines felt themselves threatened by the Separatists they tended to strengthen the power of synods. But whether or not the Dissenting Brethren became more Independent and less synodical, that was not originally their position. They believed that a synod *did* mediate the power and authority of Jesus Christ among equals; but it was among *equals,* and in the final issue if the views of a local church and a synod seemed to disagree regarding the affairs of that local congregation, the balance must remain in the local covenanted church where the preaching of the Word, the administration of regular sacraments, and pastoral care provided the context within which church discipline should be properly exercised.

Robert Baillie was one of the keenest observers of the Dissenting Brethren, and his reports of the main differences between them and the views that he represented are models of clarity. In one of his letters to his cousin appealing for help from the Reformed theologians on the continent of Europe he gave an excellent summary of the main points at issue:

> The chief point we wish were proven, is the real authoritie, power, and jurisdiction of Synods and classical Presbyteries over any of the members, or the whole of a particular congregation; also the right of ordinarie professors to the sacrament, though they can give no certaine or satisfactorie signes of reall regeneration. These two are the main heads; also I wish that the power of Presbyteries classical, to ordaine and excommunicate, were cleared. Many besides the Independents, by Voetius's writes, are brought to give the rights of both these actions to the congregationall presbytery, much against our mind and practice. . . . Also, it's a great question about the power of jurisdiction in a congregation. We are not against the people's power of election of the officers, or, at least, free consent thereto; but beside, they presse all processe and acts of censures to be done, if not in the name and authoritie, as the Brownists, and these of New England, yet necessarilie in the presence, and with the consent, not only of the presbyterie congregationall, but also of the whole people, even every communicant male. If in these we were agreed, I think the difficulty would be small in any other matter.[8]

---

[8] To Spang, 12th July, 1644, *Letters and Journals,* II: 205. Baillie also gave other excellent summaries of the Independents' view in his letters to Spang, 25th October, 1644, and to Buchanan, [n.d.], *Ibid.,* pp. 236, 252–53.

The crucial matter was that of spiritual jurisdiction, and by whom it was to be exercised, and it came to a head in the claim (or in the denial) that a synod had the right to excommunicate. Alexander Henderson made his plea for a private conference with the Independents early in 1645 because he had heard some of them exclaim that if they could obtain satisfaction on this matter, no basic difference would remain; but almost a year earlier Philip Nye, in commenting how near he and his colleagues came to the Presbyterian position, had pointed out that the fundamental question was whether the presbytery (or synod) was to have equal power to that of *ecclesia prima,* the local church.[9]

3. *The Basic Issue.*

Was this simply a question of church government and polity? Was the power of the local congregation, as *ecclesia prima,* the real point at issue, or did it not involve something much deeper — the nature of spiritual authority itself? In one of the debates Nye had declared that just as the administration of the sacraments was a matter of authority and not one of jurisdiction, so " our debates here are of authority but not of jurisdiction."[10]

What did he mean by this? From the context it is clear that he was speaking not about the Assembly's position vis-à-vis Parliament, because the debate was about the church at Jerusalem. Surely he was maintaining that in these debates the Assembly was fundamentally concerned with spiritual authority and not with ecclesiastical jurisdiction. He was making the same kind of distinction that Thomas Goodwin made later when he argued that the action of the Jerusalem Council was " persuasive, and not authoritative."[11] The terms are confused, but the two men meant the same thing and were making the same distinction. What Nye described as " jurisdiction " Goodwin thought of as " authoritative " in the sense that " an act of government " is authoritative — a distinction which is clear if the whole of his speech is read.[12] If we are to

---

[9] 12th February, 1644, Lightfoot, *Journal,* p. 144.

[10] 13th February, 1644, *Ibid.,* p. 150.

[11] 12th March, 1644, *Ibid.,* p. 209.

[12] The Dissenting Brethren use the word " authoritative " in precisely this way in the *Apologeticall Narration.* Cf. what they say about Presbyterial government, p. 24, with what they say about excommunication and the State's involvement in it, p. 18–19.

understand the principle that they were haltingly trying to enunciate we must get behind the confusion of words to the idea that lay behind. It is the distinction between the authority of persuasion *in* the Gospel, and (the common error of every established Church) enforced obedience *because of* the Gospel's authority.

We must be careful not to drive the point too hard. The Congregationalists themselves often lost sight of this principle in their anxiety to follow literally the Biblical pattern of their way, and yet we catch the glimmer of an insight about the nature of spiritual authority which is still of primary importance in our understanding of the Church.

Later writers were to speak of this as the distinction between " magisterial " and " ministerial " power. The former was the kind of power that was proper to the civil magistrate, and it was ultimately backed by the force and coercion which the State could command; but the latter was proper to the Church, and it was backed by the inherent authority of the Word of God and persuasion in the truth. Or, to put it in an axiom that might do duty for us today: *the authority which Jesus Christ gives to his Church is His authority only as it is exercised in the spirit of Jesus Christ.* The place of this insight in the thinking of the seventeenth-century Congregationalists may be seen as we consider its effects upon their conception of the Church.

(1) At its root, the insistence upon the primacy of the local covenanted congregation rested upon their assertion that the kerygmatic and sacramental ministry in the church and the pastoral jurisdiction or discipline in the church must be held together. They were distinct functions within the church but they belonged to the *church,* in its wholeness. Stephen Marshall had been quite right when he had demanded that " The thing to be proved is that a Synodical Assembly is a ministerial Church,"[13] for under the pressure of the Presbyterian attack Independents sometimes tended to slight the pastoral aspects of a synod's function. Furthermore, the literalistic exegesis of their own time often forced them into justifying the local church as *ecclesia prima* without asking how this

---

[13] March 3rd, 1644/5, *The Minutes of the Sessions of the Westminster Assembly of Divines* (William Blackwood & Sons, Edinburgh, 1874, edited by A. F. Mitchell and J. Struthers), p. 66.

might be modified by the universality and the spirit of the New Testament as a whole. As it was, however, the fundamental point which they were making about the relationship of ministry to spiritual authority was never really met by the Assembly, for their plea was that jurisdiction within the Church of Jesus Christ could be exercised properly only within the framework of a ministry — a pastoral ministry, exercised pastorally : the claim to the Keys was valid only within a community that had also put itself corporately under the discipline of discovering the mind of Christ in Word and Sacrament.

(2) It affected too their understanding of synods. To the Congregationalist of the seventeenth century a synod possessed real spiritual authority, as Baillie understood very well. " They avow a dependencie, and that by Divine command, on all the neighbour churches; only denyes a superioritie of jurisdiction of any church or synod over another church." This denial of " jurisdiction " does not mean that the synod had no right to admonish or even to command in the name of Christ, but it meant that the synod had no right to excommunicate or to legislate in such a way that an individual church would be no longer a church. When they were not reacting too strongly against Presbyterianism they recognized that there was real spiritual authority in the synod. Jeremiah Burroughes wrote, " Synods of other ministers and Elders about them are an ordinance of Jesus Christ for the helping of the Church against errors, schismes, and scandals," and he continued, " these Synods may be [by] the power they have from Christ admonish men or Churches in his name . . . and their admonition carry with them the authority of Jesus Christ." Further, a synod might declare these errant individuals or churches to be subverters of the Faith, might refuse communion with them until they repent, and in the final resort, he asserted, " they may declare, and that also in the name of Christ that these erring people or Churches, are not to be received into the fellowship with any of the Churches of Christ, nor have communion with another in the ordinances of Christ."[14]

Certainly here " historic " Congregationalism, even of the English " Independent " variety, goes considerably beyond what many modern Congregationalists would recognize by that name. Over

---

[14] *Irenicum*, p. 42f.

against his Presbyterian neighbor the seventeenth-century Congregationalist did not deny that the synod mediated spiritual authority, but only that it could not properly exercise coercive power. The very nature of its authority meant that there was a necessary limit to its power, even its spiritual power, because it was not equipped to exert a full ministry, complete in itself. Therefore, no synod could " unchurch " a covenanted church — it might admonish, exhort, and even separate from it, but it could not cast it off as of no account to Jesus Christ. "And what further authority, or proceedings purely Ecclesiasticall, of one, or many sister Churches towards another whole Church, or Churches offending, either the Scriptures doe hold forth, or can rationally be put into execution . . . ," declared the Apologists, " for our parts we saw not then, nor doe yet see."[15]

Excommunication was the Church's last sentence upon an erring brother. With that mixture of seventeenth-century literalism and forward-looking insight into New Testament truth which is so tantalizing when one reads their words, they concluded that it was to be exercised by the local congregation alone, because this was the place where excommunication was jurisdiction within the context of Ministry. It was so awesome a sentence, and the Church's power in it was so absolute, that it was to be used only in extreme cases upon adamant impenitence,[16] and this, they thought, only the ongoing covenanted community of faith and worship could judge. And even when it was invoked, it broke the ties and asserted the Church's separation from sin, so that it might work contrition in the erring member and reclaim him from the lost.

(3) The principle had an equally direct reference to the question of toleration in matters of religion. In Burroughes's desire to emphasize the closeness of his views with those of the Assembly, he declared that they " who are for a Congregationall way, doe not hold an absolute liberty for all religions,"[17] for the devil was not to

---

[15] *Supra* p. 17.

[16] Cotton Mather notes, for example, that during Thomas Hooker's fourteen years at Hartford only one person was admonished and one person excommunicated. This did not arise out of any lack of concern for the purity of the church, but only from the extreme seriousness with which Hooker regarded the sentence of excommunication. Mather, *Magnalia* (1855), I: 349.

[17] *Irenicum,* p. 41.

be left alone even when he invaded men's consciences.[18] However, he went on to say that the " onely way the Church hath to keep downe errors or heresies is spirituall "[19] : there must be no coercion. " We would have no coative violence used against such men who carry themselves religiously and peaceably in their differences," he said, " in such things onely as godly and peaceable men may doe and differ in."[20]

This implied an important limitation on the extent to which the Church should invoke the power of the civil magistrate. " Will you call in his power in all matters of difference, wherein you cannot agree? " he asked, " or will you desire his power to help, when either the hainousnesse of the matter, or the turbulencie of the carriage, manifests stubbornnesse? If in the former case then you make the Magistrate the Judge of all Controversies in Religion, which I believe you are not willing to do. If in the latter onely, we are agreed."[21]

Of course, it would remain a moot point as to what constituted " turbulencie of the carriage " or " stubbornnesse," but they had glimpses of a New Testament principle that would eventually undercut the very basis on which the policy of unity through coercion in Church and State had been built. The Presbyterians in the Assembly thought that to rob the Church of its right to invoke the civil power was to rob Jesus Christ[22] of his lawful authority, but Burroughes argued in the Assembly that " It's honour enough to governors that they look to the worship of God, that it be observed *according to the mind of Christ* "[23]; fundamentally that which is contrary to the spirit of Jesus could not be according to the mind of Christ. In other words, to put our axiom now in a negative way : *to exercise the authority of Jesus Christ in a way that is contrary to His spirit, is to invalidate that very authority which is claimed.*

---

[18] *Ibid.,* p. 29.

[19] *Ibid.,* p. 42.

[20] *Vindication of Mr. Burroughes, Against Mr. Edwards,* p. 28.

[21] *Ibid.,* p. 30.

[22] Cf. the remarks by Herle and Calamy in the debate on February 13th, 1645, *Minutes,* pp. 56–57.

[23] 21st February 1645, *Ibid.,* p. 63 ; the italics are mine.

It makes a good deal of difference to the reading of church history when one reviews the Church's claims about itself in the light of this principle.

* * * * *

Historians reviewing the theological disputes of the seventeenth century may very well differ in what they select as the Congregationalists' fundamental or most basic insight into the nature of the Church. Often it has been interpreted primarily in terms of polity or practice — ecclesiastical " democracy," or the principle of the " Church Meeting " — and at other times in terms of the constitution of the covenanted church itself as a gathered fellowship of " visible saints." Or we might select their claim to freedom in the interpretation of the Biblical rule — that " second principle " which the Apologists took to themselves, never to make their present judgment " a binding law " and to maintain their liberty to change " what ever should be discovered to be taken up out of a misunderstanding of the rule."[24] More properly, as we have recently been reminded,[25] any serious attempt to explore and understand their concept of the church will discover that all these elements had their place.

However, the modern Christian, concerned for the Church in an ecumenical age, can no more reproduce exactly the church forms of the seventeenth century than the Christians of Cromwell's time (despite their sanguine hopes) could produce a facsimile of the Apostolic era. We are forced to ask what there was within their particular insights which could be of abiding importance for the Church. It is a task beyond that of historical interpretation, but without which history itself has little significance.

When we look beyond the Independents' immediate demands in polity and practice, which were so often drawn from the literal Biblical pattern, we discover that they were beginning to say something of supreme importance about the nature of authority in the Church. In common with all other " churches " they asserted that the authority of the Church was the authority of Jesus Christ himself. As Thomas Goodwin was to write later, the Church is

---

[24] *Supra* p. 10f.
[25] E.g. in Dr. G. F. Nuttall's *Visible Saints.*

constituted by the authority of Jesus Christ,[26] and he went on to say that the Church also possessed that authority and exercised it. " Power spiritual," he said in his somewhat abstruse prose, " is an impress of, or an investiture with, the authority of Christ, merely out of his will, whereby men are authorized and enabled by commission from Christ, and in his name, to do what others cannot do; and by virtue of which what they so do hath a special efficacy in it from the power of Christ, seconding it and accompanying of it; which also the conscience acknowledging subjects itself to, as unto the power of Christ, for the sake of his will and institution."[27] Goodwin and his friends did not lessen the claim of the Church to her Christ-given authority. Almost all churches in the seventeenth century, however, had gone on to infer that to oppose the Church was to oppose Christ, and therefore that the State in the Church's name was justified in bringing against such disobedience the full rigor of its secular power. Every inquisition that has been launched has been promoted on the assumption of the Church's God-given authority.

We must stress that this was the formative period of Congregationalism, and the implications of their insistence upon New Testament authority for church life and practice were not yet understood fully, even by the wisest among them. Even at this time they were struggling between the letter of the New Testament and the Spirit of the New Testament, and it was not yet certain which principle would become supreme in their thinking. They were feeling their way for a truth that perhaps they saw only dimly, but which they had nevertheless begun to see. They agreed that the Church's authority had been given it by Christ, and they agreed that to oppose it was sin, but their departure was in the tacit assertion that this authority which comes from Christ could be His authority only as it was exercised in His spirit, ministerially, according to His mind. This was the reason for insisting that spiritual jurisdiction could be performed within the context of the Church's life of worship and pastoral care, and this was the reason for insisting that the only censures that were appropriate to the Church were spirit-

---

[26] *On the Constitution, Right-Order, and Government of the Churches of Christ, Works,* XI: 7–8.

[27] *Ibid.*, p. 22.

ual: the Church could not invoke the use of force without denying the very authority she claimed, and the Church could not exercise spiritual jurisdiction except as an expression of its ministry, and in fulfillment of the same. As John Cotton declared in his foreword to Norton's *Responsio,* "Church government is not an authority but a ministry."

This principle, that the authority of Jesus Christ must be exercised in the spirit of Jesus Christ, remains at the heart of the ecumenical problem. We still often confuse authority in the Church with ecclesiastical power, and if dungeon, torture and faggot are no longer regarded as respectable means for the Church to use in asserting the authority given to her by Jesus Christ, ecclesiastical power structures are still not unknown to us. Moreover, we need to give some thought to the possibility that even " spiritual " censures may be exercised in a way that is a complete denial of the Spirit of Jesus Christ.

By emphasizing that the government of the Church ought always to be according to the mind of Christ, the Congregationalists of the seventeenth century were protesting against these wrong conceptions of authority in the Church. They therefore help us to discern a principle of very great ecumenical importance. It may be too much to ask that the Dissenting Brethren and their colleagues should have been able to isolate this basic New Testament principle from their literal interpretation of Scripture and the restorationist polity that was inherent in that; but if they had managed to do this and had succeeded in getting it accepted, they need not have feared presbyteries, bishops, or for that matter, even a pope.

Bibliographical Note

A PART from Thomas Edwards's *Antapologia* there are no books that deal with the *Apologeticall Narration* itself and, as we have indicated, very little biographical material about its authors. Yet the *Apologeticall Narration* and those responsible for it touched history in three significant areas: the English Civil War; the course of the Westminster Assembly; and the historical development of Congregationalism.

With regard to the first of these we can only direct the serious student to the basic authorities of the Civil War period, some of which appear dispersed among the footnotes of the preceding essay. To say anything about the bibliography of the English Civil War invites criticism, because this period has been covered more extensively than any other in English history. But we can perhaps make the point that beyond the general histories of the period (S. R. Gardiner, C. H. Firth, C. V. Wedgwood, *et al.*) interesting biographical sidelights on some of the lesser known personalities must be sought among the Memoir writers, and in the amorphous masses of anecdote, eulogy and scandal in a book like Wood's *Athenae Oxonienses*. Wood is the perfect epitome of Carlyle's pet phobia, "Dryasdust," but he and his kind provide us with the stuff of which the history of the period was made.

Turning more specifically to the history of the Westminster Assembly, we find some surprising *lacunae*. The Minutes of the Assembly are nowhere available to us in a complete and well-edited form, and although there is a plethora of those who write *about* the Assembly and its work, very few have been prepared to wrestle with the incredibly complex task of unraveling the details of procedure to give us a straightforward account of what happened, when, and in what sequence.

The debates of the Assembly are most readily available to us in John Lightfoot's *The Journal of the Proceedings of the Assembly of Divines, from January 1, 1643, to December 31, 1644* (edited by the Revd. John R. Pitman, and published in 1824 as Vol. XIII of

Lightfoot's *Works*) and *The Minutes of the Sessions of the West-minster Assembly of Divines* (edited by A. F. Mitchell and J. Struthers, and published in Edinburgh in 1874). Unfortunately, the latter work covers the period only from Session 324 to Session 1163, i.e., from November 18th, 1644, to February 22nd, 1648, and it therefore omits entirely the most important and interesting portion of the Assembly's debates, which occurred from the middle of October 1643 through 1644. Moreover these *Minutes* are simply the rough notes and jottings of someone in the Assembly who was not interested in taking down a full précis of the argument and seems to have had difficulty in hearing the major part of the discussion. The *Minutes* are of limited usefulness.

John Lightfoot's *Journal* is of far more value, since it covers the very important period January–December, 1644, when the issues between the Presbyterians and the Independents were being thrashed out. It is not absolutely complete, for sometimes Lightfoot was absent from the debates, but the writer provides us with a fairly good summary of what was said. Lightfoot is testy and cryptic, and often obscure, but one has the sense of reading a first-hand account of the Assembly; and at any rate his Erastian prejudices enable him to be equally opposed to Scottish Presbyterian pressures and to Independent filibustering.

As a supplement to this we have another eyewitness account in the *Letters and Journals* of Robert Baillie, the Scottish Commissioner. This is a mine of information, and since Baillie is writing to his own friends he is extremely frank in his comments, not only about his opponents but also about the motives and methods of the Scottish Commissioners. Furthermore, although he openly reveals his Scottish and Presbyterian prejudices (to him they were identical) he is rarely if ever unfair to the views of an opponent, and his accounts of the Assembly's work are models of clarity. We wish he had been appointed Scribe.

One of the most recent books *about* the Assembly is Dr. S. W. Carruther's *The Everyday Work of the Westminster Assembly* (1943). It contains many valuable insights into questions such as the relationship between the Assembly and Parliament, but it would have been of more value if it had included a concise and accurate chronological account of the Assembly's work, for although the doctrinal and liturgical matters with which the Assembly

128

dealt have often been treated by "masters of their subjects," they often leave their readers more than a little vague about the actual sequence of events. A similar criticism can be leveled at Professor Benjamin B. Warfield's *The Westminster Assembly and its Work* (1931) since only the first chapter deals specifically with this subject and the great debates of 1644 are hardly mentioned. Of the rest, in 1841 the Presbyterian Board of Publication published *A History of the Westminster Assembly* which gives some useful biographical information about members of the Assembly, but the best account of the Assembly is that of the Revd. W. M. Hetherington, *A History of the Westminister Assembly* (1843). It is quite outrageous in the naively flagrant prejudices of its author, which represent the Scottish Commissioners as models of Christian probity in a welter of English Independent Machiavellianism, but beyond this bias the author knew his sources, honestly grappled with the intricacies of his subject, and has therefore given us one of the clearest accounts of the Assembly's work in a proper sequence.

To give a complete account of the *Apologeticall Narration's* bibliographical relationship to Congregational history would demand a booklet at least the size of the pamphlet itself. One cannot do better than direct the serious reader to the titles in the invaluable bibliography of H. M. Dexter's *The Congregationalism of the Last Three Hundred Years* (1880). The list is not as exhaustive as its compiler believed, but it is the best bibliography of its kind and demands to be republished in a revised and supplemented form.

In the course of recent research it can be shown that the great debate between the Presbyterians and the Congregationalists contains within it several distinct literary debates between individuals. The controversy became truly trans-Atlantic.[1]

It began with the *Thirty-two Questions* sent over by a group of Presbyterians in 1637 and answered by Richard Mather from New England two years later. It gathered impetus in the *Apologeticall Narration* and the debates of the Assembly, and in the literary

---

[1] In an unpublished thesis submitted for the degree of Ph.D., the Reverend Richard A. Hasler has managed to distinguish seven distinct literary debates within the major Presbyterian-Congregational discussion. Cf. *The Concept of the Ministry in Puritan New England, as exemplified in the Life and Thought of Thomas Shepard (1605–1649)* (Hartford Seminary Foundation), pp. 56ff.

discussion that developed between Charles Herle (*The Independency on the Scriptures of the Independency of Churches,* 1643) and Samuel Rutherford (*Due Right of Presbyteries,* 1644), on the Presbyterian side, with Richard Mather on the Congregational side (*Modest & Brotherly Answer to Mr. Charles Herle His Book,* 1644 and *A Reply to Mr. Rutherford*). Other debates that went on within the same general discussion involved Apollonius' *Consideratio* (1645) and John Norton's *Responsio* (1648), Rutherford's *Due Right of Presbyteries* and Hooker's *A Survey of the Summe of Church Discipline,* Robert Baillie's *Dissuasive* and John Cotton's *The Way of the Congregational Churches Cleared,* and a further debate which began with the *Nine Propositions* of 1637 and ended with Thomas Shepard and John Allin's *A Defence of the Answer.* This demonstrates something of the literary ramifications that were thrown up by the Congregational-Presbyterian debate, in which the *Apologeticall Narration* occupied a pivotal position, but the list is by no means exhaustive. A thorough survey of all the books related to the appearance of this pamphlet would lead us into a comprehensive bibliography of the doctrine of the church in seventeenth-century Congregationalism and to the subsequent writings of the Apologists.

The one book that deals specifically with the *Apologeticall Narration* is the *Antapologia* (1644). It does not attempt to tell us how the pamphlet came to be written, but it is a full length vitriolic attack on the claims of the Dissenting Brethren by means of an extensive commentary on the text. It does not help us very much to appraise the value of the *Apologeticall Narration,* but it does provide us with the background events of the Apologists' previous history through the eyes of one who cordially detested the view of the Church that they represented. And the fact that Edwards dignified this pamphlet with over 300 pages of commentary within a year of its appearance, pays an unconscious tribute to its influence at that time.

Index

References to the actual text of *An Apologeticall Narration* are to the first thirty-one pages and are indicated by parentheses, e.g. (1).

Authors listed in the Index include only those mentioned in the text itself or commented upon in the footnotes.

Congregationalism, (1–31) *passim,*
64, 82; "The Congregational Way,"
34, 43, 45–47, 52n, Chapter II *passim,* 83–84, 100, 102, 104, 110n, 113–
14; Church, doctrine of, 45–59,
Chapter V *passim;* Church meeting, 86; Church polity, 115–18;
Elders, 37–39; English Classis in
Netherlands, 60, 84; Excommunication, 121; Synods, 120–21; Visible Saints, 35, 38; Worship, 114–15.
Cotton, John, 39, 49, 52, 55, 59, 64n,
83–85, 85n, 90, 96, 110n, 125, 130.
Crawford, Laurence, 75, 79–80.
Cromwell, Henry, 88.
Cromwell, Oliver, 51n, 54, 60, 75–
80, 86–88, 94–95, 101, 103, 123.
Cromwell, Richard, 95.
Cudworth, Ralph, 88n.

DAVENPORT, John, 59, 84, 110n.
de la War, Lord, see Thomas West.
Devereux, Robert, Earl of Essex, 69,
74, 75.
Dexter, H. M., 59n, 128.
Dissenting Brethren, see Independen-
dency.
Dury, John, 53n, 107n.

ECUMENISM, 53n, 66, 123–25.
Edwards, Thomas, 40–41, 50, 82, 90,
97–99, 102–104, 126, 129.
"Ejector," 85, 93.
Elders, see Congregationalism.
Eliot, John, 109n.
Elizabeth I, Queen of England, 57.
English Classis in Netherlands, see
Congregationalism.
Episcopacy, 36, 44, 54n, Chapter II
passim, 69–70, 98; Book of Com-
mon Prayer, 70; Book of Sports,
104.
Essex, Earl of, see Robert Devereux.
Excommunication, see Congrega-
tionalism.

FEATLEY, Daniel, 44, 92, 92n.
Fiennes, William, Lord Saye and
Sele, 61n.
Fifth Monarchists, 69, 95–96.
Firth, C. H., 126.
Fitz, Richard, 63.
Forbes, Alexander, 100.
Fuller, Thomas, 45, 81, 81n, 83.

GALE, Theophilus, 86.
Gardiner, S. R., 72n, 126.
Goodwin, John, 78, 96.
Goodwin, Thomas, Biographical
Note, 83–89; mentioned also 55,
65n, 68, Chapter IV *passim,* 118,
123.
Gordon, Alexander, 96.
Green, John, 109.
Greenhill, William, 81, 105, 108n, 109.
Guicciardini, Ludovico, (7), 36.

HAMPDEN, John, 74, 78.
Harrison, Robert, 35.
Heads of Agreement (1691), 55–56.
Henderson, Alexander, 118.
Herle, Charles, 33, 122n, 129.
Hetherington, W. M., 128.
Heylyn, Peter, 37.
Holles, Denzil, 74.
Hooker, Thomas, 49, 55, 62n, 84, 85n,
108n, 109n, 110n, 121n, 129.
Horton, Douglas, 48n, 64n.
Howe, John, 86.
Hutchinson, Anne, 92, 110n.

INDEPENDENCY, see the text of
An Apologeticall Narration and
Notes *passim;* see all references to
Congregationalism; Dissenting
Brethren, 62n, 65, 67, 73, 79–80,
Chapter IV *passim,* 117–18, 125;
English Independents, Chapter I
passim; New England Puritans,
Chapter I *passim.*